USBORNE
OUR WORLD

I See a reb

Ella MoM Ella Ella

Ella Ella

Ella

Ella S

D1275332

USBORNE
OUR WORLD

Flid

SCHOLASTIC INC.

New York   Toronto   London   Auckland   Sydney

ISBN 0-590-92186-X

"Ecology" copyright © 1994, 1988 by Usborne Publishing Ltd.
"Planet Earth" copyright © 1991 by Usborne Publishing Ltd.
All rights reserved. Published by Scholastic Inc., 555 Broadway, New York, NY 10012,
by arrangement with Usborne Publishing Ltd.

12 11 10 9 8 7 6 5 4 3 2 1   7 8 9/9 0 1 2/0

Printed in the U.S.A.

First Scholastic printing, February 1997

CONTENTS

USBORNE
OUR WORLD

BOOK ONE
ECOLOGY

Richard Spurgeon

Edited by Corinne Stockley

Designed by Stephen Wright

Illustrated by
Kuo Kang Chen, Brin Edwards and Caroline Ewen

Scientific advisor: Dr. Margaret Rostron

Contents

About this book

Ecology is the study of all living things and how they work with each other and the world around them. This book shows how plants, animals and their environments are all linked together in one vast web, and how we ourselves are all part of this web. It explains the basic terms and ideas of ecology, using examples from the very different ecological regions of the world.

Throughout this book, there are many examples of how the things people are doing today are causing problems and disturbances in the natural world. At the same time, there are suggestions as to what can be done to help. These range from activities which will help you improve the situation in your local area, to some ideas about how the larger scale problems could be solved.

Using the glossary

The glossary on pages 46-47 is a useful reference point. It brings together and explains all the main ecological terms used in the book.

Useful addresses

If you want to get more involved in helping wildlife and improving the environment, or just want to find out more about what other people are doing, you can turn to pages 44-45. These have a list of addresses of leading conservation and environmental groups. Many of these organizations run activities for young people, and all of them will send you more information.

This scene shows one of the harshest of the world's environments, and some of the people and animals adapted to survive there. You can find out more about the ecology of the world's deserts on pages 16-17.

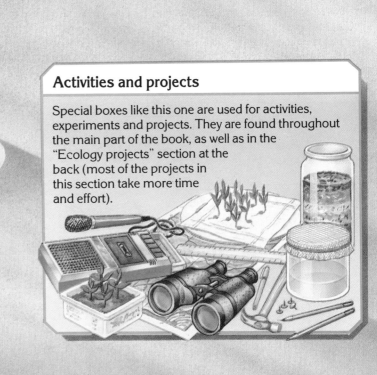

Activities and projects

Special boxes like this one are used for activities, experiments and projects. They are found throughout the main part of the book, as well as in the "Ecology projects" section at the back (most of the projects in this section take more time and effort).

What is ecology?

Ecology is the study of living things in their natural surroundings, or **environment**. This is everything, living and non-living, that is around them.

Your own environment is made up of all that you can see and much that you can't when you look around you. Its basic features stay very much the same, e.g. the air that you breathe, but the details are constantly changing.

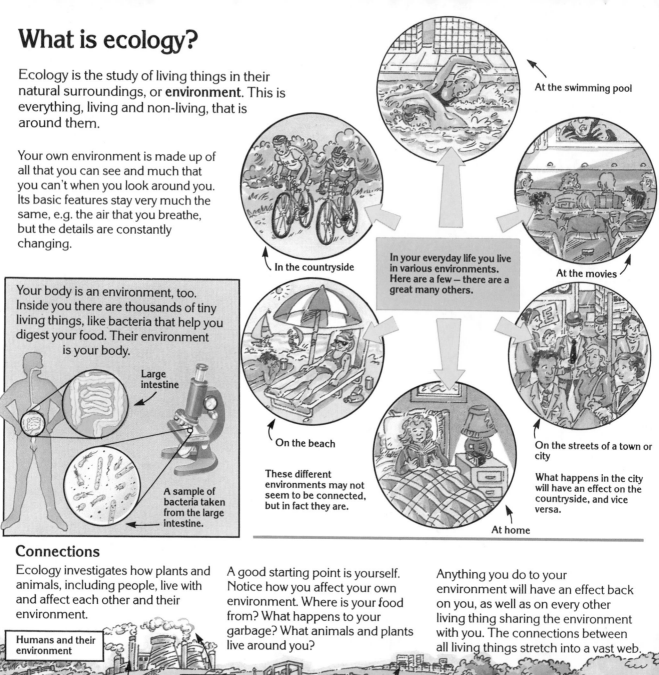

Your body is an environment, too. Inside you there are thousands of tiny living things, like bacteria that help you digest your food. Their environment is your body.

Large intestine

A sample of bacteria taken from the large intestine.

In your everyday life you live in various environments. Here are a few — there are a great many others.

At the swimming pool

In the countryside

At the movies

On the beach

These different environments may not seem to be connected, but in fact they are.

At home

On the streets of a town or city

What happens in the city will have an effect on the countryside, and vice versa.

Connections

Ecology investigates how plants and animals, including people, live with and affect each other and their environment.

A good starting point is yourself. Notice how you affect your own environment. Where is your food from? What happens to your garbage? What animals and plants live around you?

Anything you do to your environment will have an effect back on you, as well as on every other living thing sharing the environment with you. The connections between all living things stretch into a vast web.

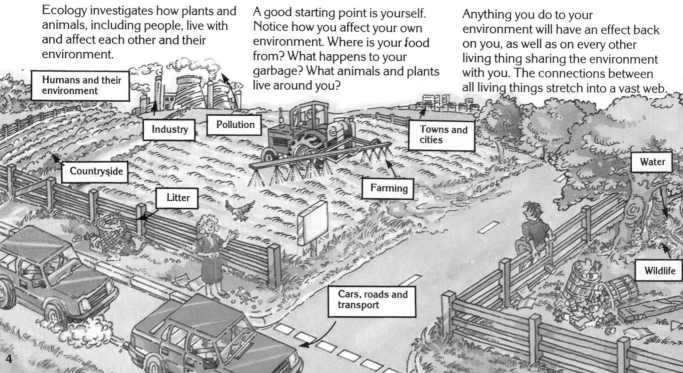

Humans and their environment

Industry

Pollution

Towns and cities

Countryside

Water

Litter

Farming

Wildlife

Cars, roads and transport

Habitats

The natural home of a group of plants and animals is called a **habitat** and the group of plants and animals which live there is a **community**. Lift up a stone and see what lives in the habitat underneath it.

Smaller habitats are part of larger habitats. The stone may be at the side of a stream, which may be in a wood. A different, larger community lives in each larger habitat.

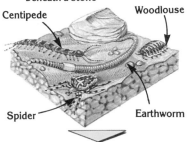

Community of animals living beneath a stone

Centipede
Woodlouse
Spider
Earthworm

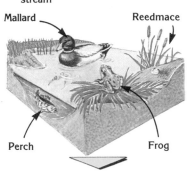

Part of community living by or in a stream

Mallard
Reedmace
Perch
Frog

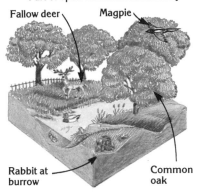

Part of open woodland community

Fallow deer
Magpie
Rabbit at burrow
Common oak

Try to find some different habitats in your area. Look everywhere – in, on, under and around. But remember to leave everything as you found it.

A freshwater pond

A pond is a good example of a larger habitat. It is the home of a large community of different plants and animals. The pond, its community, and the non-living environment around it, make up a complete ecological unit, called an **ecosystem**. For more on ecosystems and how they work, see page 8.

Pond-dipping is a good way of studying the pond community. Gently drag a net through different areas of the pond. Make notes on what you find. Put anything interesting into a container for closer inspection (you could use a book on pond life for identification). Don't forget to put everything back into the pond when you have finished.

You can either buy a net or make your own. Get a metal coat-hanger and bend it into a circle. Stick the ends into a long piece of bamboo, or tie them to a pole, and tie an old stocking to the rim.

A home-made net

Tie a knot in the stocking and cut off the excess.

Tie the stocking to the rim with string.

Ponds are much less common today than they were forty years ago. Many have been filled in or have grown over. This is most unfortunate for their inhabitants. Some plants and animals only live in certain habitats. When these disappear, so do they.

Build your own pond

You can help the wildlife in your area by building a pond. This will attract all sorts of wildlife and is not too hard to do. See pages 36-37 for instructions on how to make, stock and maintain a pond.

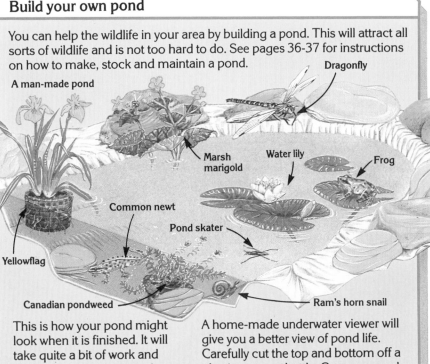

A man-made pond

Dragonfly
Marsh marigold
Water lily
Frog
Common newt
Pond skater
Yellowflag
Canadian pondweed
Ram's horn snail

This is how your pond might look when it is finished. It will take quite a bit of work and time, and must be properly looked after, but once it is established many animals will come to visit or stay and you will be able to study them whenever you want.

A home-made underwater viewer will give you a better view of pond life. Carefully cut the top and bottom off a plastic squeezy bottle. Cover one end with clear plastic wrap and attach it with a rubber band. Place it in the water and look through the open end (for safety, cover the cut edge with tape).

Underwater viewer

The environment

As well as influencing our environment, we are constantly being influenced by it. Like all living things, we are dependent on our environment for the essentials of life.

The basis of all life on earth is the sun. Without its heat the world would be a frozen mass of lifeless rock and ice. It provides plants and animals with the energy they need to live. It generates the winds by heating the earth's land masses and the air above them, and drives the water cycle by evaporating water into the atmosphere (see page 12). It is the most vital component of the environment, without which life on earth could not exist.

The climate

This map shows the world's six major climates. The main influences on the climate are: distance from the Equator, distance from the ocean (it is drier inland), and the height above sea level (the higher you go, the colder it gets)

The sun's energy is not evenly spread across the surface of the earth. Equatorial areas receive far more than polar areas. This imbalance creates and drives the winds around the world.

At the poles, the sun's rays pass through more atmosphere and are spread over a larger land surface than at the Equator, so it is much colder.

The interactions of warm winds and ocean currents from the tropical areas and cold winds and currents from polar regions cause climatic variations wherever they converge.

Living things are greatly affected by the conditions around them. The temperature, rainfall and other aspects of the climate in an area influence the forms, growth and behavior of the plants and animals found there (see map on page 8).

The climate and the earth's landscape interact to create the larger environment within which life can exist. Over time, the powerful weathering effects of the climate have formed the earth's life-supporting soil.

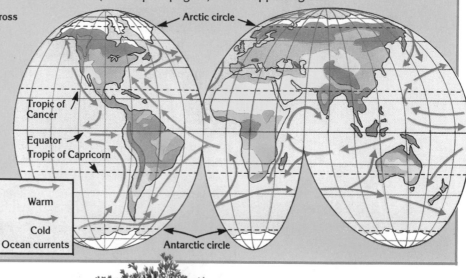

Climate key
- Polar
- Mountain
- Cold forest
- Temperate
- Dry
- Equatorial
- Sub-equatorial

Warm
Cold
Ocean currents

Arctic circle
Tropic of Cancer
Equator
Tropic of Capricorn
Antarctic circle

The importance of soil

The weathering effects of temperature, wind and water break down the rocks of the earth's surface to produce mineral particles which are the basis of soil. For more about the changing landscape, see page 28.

Tiny plants grow on these rock particles, die and decompose to form organic matter called **humus**. This mixture of mineral particles and organic matter is what makes up soil. Soil also contains water and air, trapped between the particles, and millions of microscopic organisms, like bacteria, as well as insects and some larger animals.

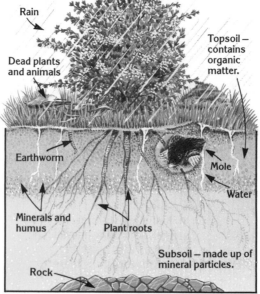

Rain
Dead plants and animals
Topsoil – contains organic matter.
Earthworm
Mole
Water
Minerals and humus
Plant roots
Subsoil – made up of mineral particles.
Rock

There are many types of soil, each with a different ratio of humus and minerals (and different types of mineral particles, formed from the breakdown of different rocks). Each type of soil supports its own range of plant species.

Soil supplies many of the essential needs of most green plants. It is the source of their water, the minerals they need to develop, and gives them a solid base in which their roots can grow.

Soil experiments

To see what soil is made of, take a sample and shake it up in a jar of water. Let it settle for a few days, then study the different layers.

Now get samples of different types of soil from a variety of places. Do the same thing to each and compare the results.

To see what sort of animals are living in the soil, take a sample and put it on a piece of gauze in a funnel. Place this on a tall jar under a lamp overnight. The light and heat will force the creatures down into the jar.

Humus – organic matter

Clay – mainly aluminum silicate

Silt – mud formed from tiny pieces of rock

Sand – mainly silica

Gravel – larger rock particles

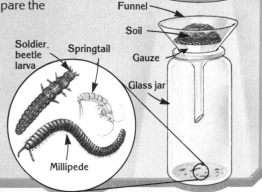

Soldier beetle larva

Springtail

Millipede

Lamp

Funnel

Soil

Gauze

Glass jar

Soil erosion

Most of the earth's surface is covered by a layer of soil, ranging from 1/4 in thick in mountainous regions to 6 1/2 ft in cultivated areas. We all depend on this thin layer for our food supplies, yet everywhere it is threatened by soil erosion.

Over-grazing, poor irrigation, intensive farming and the destruction of tree cover mean that vital topsoil is left exposed, and much is being blown or washed away. If this continues, we may not have enough fertile land left to grow enough food.

In the early 1930s, farming areas in the American mid-west were devastated by soil erosion.

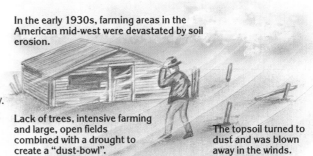

Lack of trees, intensive farming and large, open fields combined with a drought to create a "dust-bowl".

The topsoil turned to dust and was blown away in the winds.

Energy for life

All living things need energy for their growth, movement and life processes. The source of this energy is the sun.

Green plants use the sun's energy to build their own food from the simpler elements around them. They are called **producers**. They use the sunlight in a process called **photosynthesis** to convert water and carbon dioxide into oxygen and carbohydrates. Some of the carbohydrates are then combined with minerals from the soil and used for growth, others form a store of food (mainly in leaves), to provide energy when needed. Animals cannot produce their own food. They depend on the food stored in plants to give them energy for life and so are called **consumers**.

Process of photosynthesis

Cross-section of leaf

Sunlight

Chloroplasts contain chlorophyll which absorbs sunlight.

Water and minerals from roots reach leaves via veins.

Stoma (tiny opening)

Oxygen out

Carbon dioxide in

Carbohydrates made and stored in cells.

Plant experiments

Put some cress seeds in two dishes lined with damp kitchen paper. Put both in a dark cupboard for one or two days, then take one out and put it by a window. After a few more days you will see how important sunlight is for healthy plant growth.

Add some food dye to the water you give the healthy cress. Study what happens. The plants draw up the water like they would from soil.

Plants move their leaves to catch the most light. Study the growth of a plant in a sunny place, then turn it round and see what happens.

Dish from cupboard

Unhealthy cress plants

Keep the paper damp all the time.

Dish from windowsill

Healthy cress plants

Ecosystems

An ecosystem consists of a given habitat and its community. The living things within it interact with each other and their non-living (**abiotic**) environment to form an ecological unit which is largely self-contained.

Many smaller ecosystems can be found within larger ones, like a rotting tree branch, within a wood.

Biomes are the largest ecosystems into which the earth's land surface can be divided (see right). They are named after the main type of vegetation found there, and each one is home to a very large variety of plants and animals.

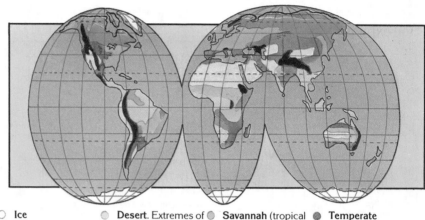

○ **Ice**

● **Mountain**

● **Maquis**. Warm, wet winters, hot, dry summers, scrubland.

○ **Tropical forest**. Hot and wet, with a great diversity of life, e.g. monkeys and exotic birds.

○ **Desert**. Extremes of temperature, little rain, scarcity of life.

● **Deciduous forest**. Warm summers, cold winters, mainly deciduous woodland (e.g. oak or beech), variety of animals.

● **Savannah** (tropical grassland) – hot with wet winters, open plains with trees, antelopes.

● **Coniferous forest**. Cold all year, dominated by forests of conifers (e.g. spruce and pine), deer and wolves.

● **Temperate grassland**. Hot summers, cold winters, open grassy plains, buffalo.

○ **Tundra**. Very cold, windy and treeless, little animal life.

The climate of each biome (see global climate map, page 6) directly influences the different types of plant and animal that live there.

Your local ecosystems

A good way to get to know the ecology of your local area is to make a map of the areas of interest. Get hold of a large scale map of your district and copy the main features like roads and buildings, or photocopy it. Then go out and survey the area, noting down the position of important ecosystems. Fill these in on your map and make a key to explain the symbols and colours that you use. Once you have made your map, keep your eyes open for interesting things to add.

Example of an ecosystem map

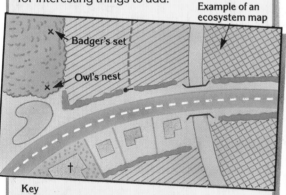

Badger's set

Owl's nest

Key

	Woodland		Pond
	Hedgerow		Building
	River or stream		Road
†	Church		Graveyard
	Wheat-field		Meadow
	Bridge	●—	Gate
×	Point of interest		Footpath

Food chains

The plants and animals in a given ecosystem are linked by their feeding relationships. The plants act as producers (see page 7) by using the sun's energy to produce food, which provides animals with the energy they need to live. The energy stored in plants as food is passed on through the community in a **food chain**. It is passed on directly to **primary consumers**, animals which eat plants, and indirectly to **secondary consumers**, animals which eat primary consumers. Other animals eat these secondary consumers and are known as **tertiary consumers**.

Each food chain also contains **decomposers**. These are bacteria, fungi and some types of insects that break down dead plant and animal matter into minerals and humus in the soil. In the process, they get their own energy for life from the food that they break down.

Decomposers at work

Find an old log and make a study of its decay. Take notes or photographs over a period of time of the different decomposers at work. How long does it take?

A decaying log

Fungi

Lichens

Food webs

Each ecosystem contains many different food chains which interlink to form a more complex **food web**. This is because animals often eat a varied diet and so play different roles in a number of food chains. Patterns of feeding also link different ecosystems. Animals from one will feed off plants and animals from another. In this way, all life on earth is interlinked in one vast, continuous web.

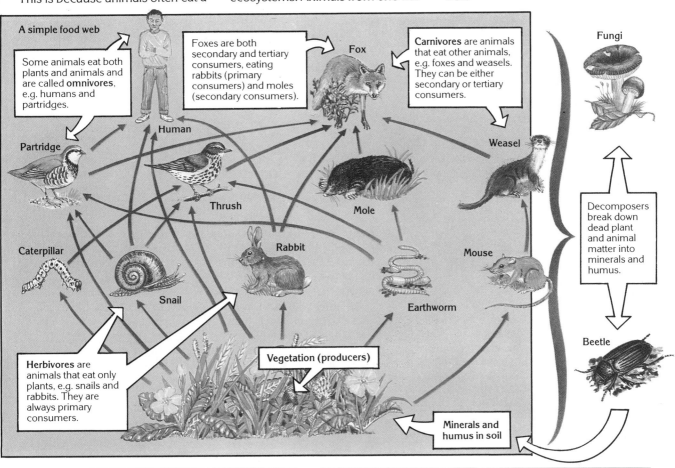

A simple food web

Some animals eat both plants and animals and are called **omnivores**, e.g. humans and partridges.

Foxes are both secondary and tertiary consumers, eating rabbits (primary consumers) and moles (secondary consumers).

Carnivores are animals that eat other animals, e.g. foxes and weasels. They can be either secondary or tertiary consumers.

Decomposers break down dead plant and animal matter into minerals and humus.

Human

Partridge

Fox

Weasel

Fungi

Thrush

Mole

Mouse

Caterpillar

Snail

Rabbit

Earthworm

Herbivores are animals that eat only plants, e.g. snails and rabbits. They are always primary consumers.

Vegetation (producers)

Beetle

Minerals and humus in soil

Constructing a food web

To show how complicated a food web can be, you can build your own. Find some old wildlife magazines, cut out pictures of individual plants and animals, and stick them onto some card. You could also trace, copy or draw them from books. Then arrange the pictures in a food web, connecting those that eat or are eaten by each other. Make different webs for different ecosystems, e.g. your local area, an African plain or the Amazon rainforest. The more pictures you find, the more complex the web will be.

String, yarn or ribbon linking pictures.

Trophic levels

Trophic levels are a way of looking at the levels in a food chain from the point of view of energy. At each level in the chain, some of the food taken in is broken down for energy and some is stored. This means that, for a given amount of food at the bottom, some is lost at each step up to a higher level, leaving less to be broken down for energy. So fewer animals can be supported at each level on that amount of food.

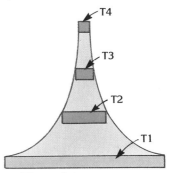

Pyramid of numbers
(number of individuals at each level)

T4
T3
T2
T1

T1 – producers
T2 – primary consumers
T3 – secondary consumers
T4 – tertiary consumers

The ocean

The oceans of the world form one vast ecosystem covering over 70% of the planet's surface. Many varied ecosystems exist within it, each with its own environment and diversity of life-forms. This vast area is little known, but it contains a wealth of resources. With more understanding and cooperation, its vast store of food, minerals and energy can be gained for the benefit of all.

These two views of the earth show the true extent of the enormous ocean ecosystem.

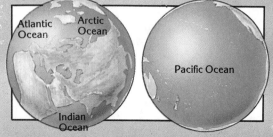

Marine habitats

The underwater landscape is just as varied as that on land, with countless different habitats and communities. There are vast areas of sandy desert, huge mountain ranges and areas rich in plant and animal life. The most spectacular of these are the tropical coral reefs. Despite existing only in relatively small areas of the vast oceans, they support a third of all fish species.

The marine food cycle

The ocean ecosystem has a vast and complicated food web (see page 9). From single-celled organisms to massive whales, the ocean is home to a range of plant and animal life that is just as diverse as that on land.

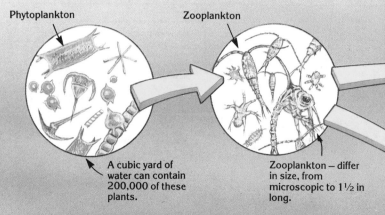

Phytoplankton

Zooplankton

A cubic yard of water can contain 200,000 of these plants.

Zooplankton – differ in size, from microscopic to 1 1/2 in long.

Almost all of the ocean's varied plant and animal life exists in the top 325 ft where sunlight can penetrate. The ocean's producers, microscopic plants called **phytoplankton**, live very close to the surface as they need the sun's energy for the process of photosynthesis. Like green plants on land, these tiny marine plants provide the basis of all life in the oceans.

Using energy absorbed from the sun, phytoplankton combine water and carbon dioxide to produce carbohydrates, the basic elements of all food webs. In the process they produce almost 70% of the world's oxygen. Phytoplankton are consumed by microscopic animals called **zooplankton**. These and other tiny creatures are eaten in turn by small fish. And so on up the food chain.

The Great Barrier Reef is one of the natural wonders of the world. Up to 170 m (500 feet) across and stretching over 2,100 km (1,260 miles) along the north-east coast of Australia, it is home to over 3,000 animal species.

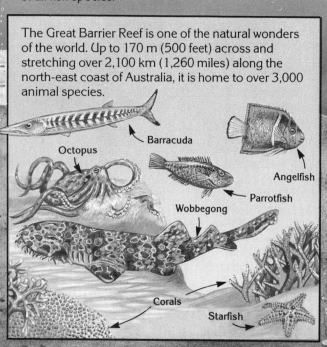

Barracuda

Octopus

Angelfish

Parrotfish

Wobbegong

Corals

Starfish

Studying plankton

If you get the chance, study a sample of seawater under a microscope. Or study water from a pond or stream – plankton live in freshwater too. The variety of life-forms is amazing. Can you find any of these common forms of plankton?

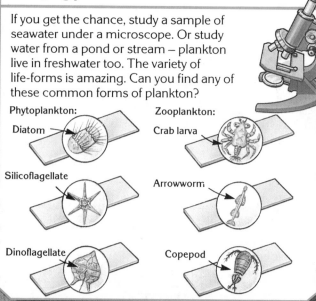

Phytoplankton:

Diatom

Silicoflagellate

Dinoflagellate

Zooplankton:

Crab larva

Arrowworm

Copepod

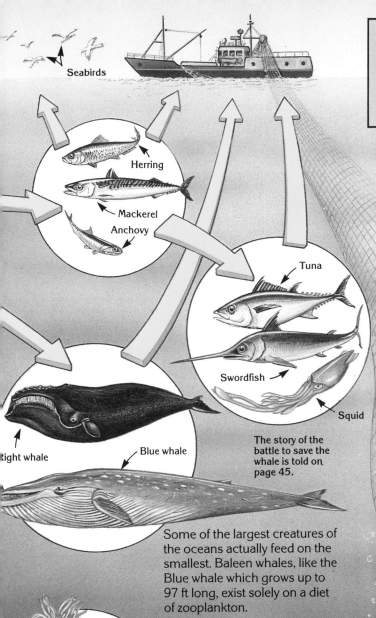

Seabirds

Herring

Mackerel

Anchovy

Tuna

Swordfish

Squid

The story of the battle to save the whale is told on page 45.

Right whale

Blue whale

Some of the largest creatures of the oceans actually feed on the smallest. Baleen whales, like the Blue whale which grows up to 97 ft long, exist solely on a diet of zooplankton.

The ocean itself plays a vital role in the earth's water cycle. Its huge surface area allows vast quantities of water to evaporate into the atmosphere. The water then condenses to form clouds (for more on the water cycle, see page 12).

Fishing

For thousands of years, man has harvested fish from the seas as a valuable food source. Today the global catch plays a vital part in feeding the world's growing population.

A fish diet?

How often do you eat fish? They are very good for you: high in protein and low in fat. Find out what sorts are available in your area, and where they come from. Have any become rarer or more expensive?

Over-fishing by large modern fishing fleets now threatens the livelihoods of traditional fishermen throughout the world. This has caused stocks of many fish species to become dangerously low. It is now vital that we have more international cooperation to sustain fish harvests.

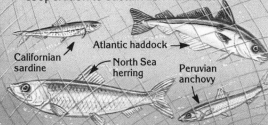

Atlantic haddock

Californian sardine

North Sea herring

Peruvian anchovy

These species have all suffered the effects of over-fishing.

Sea anemone

Swimming crab

Dead matter sinks to the ocean floor where it is either eaten by bottom dwellers (in shallower areas), like crabs and sea anemones, or it decays, producing minerals. Some form new rock, the rest are circulated by currents and taken in by plants.

Pollution

Pollution is now a major problem in marine ecosystems. Over 80% of this comes from land-based activities, e.g. sewage and industrial waste. Conditions are worst in enclosed areas like the Mediterranean and the North Sea, where levels of pollution are now so high that wildlife and human health are threatened. Measures are finally being taken to combat this international problem, but it will be a long and difficult job.

The average depth of the ocean is 4050 yds, though parts are much deeper. Even the darkest depths are not devoid of life, however – thousands of weird and wonderful creatures have adapted to life in near total darkness.

Angler fish – creates its own light to attract the smaller fish which it feeds on.

Drum containing dangerous radioactive nuclear waste dumped at sea.

11

Cycles in nature

All living things can be found within a relatively thin layer on or near the surface of the earth. Apart from the sun's energy, all their needs are supplied by the small proportion of the earth's resources contained in this layer. If the water, oxygen and other elements vital for life were only used once, they would soon run out. This is why many of nature's processes work in cycles. There is a constant exchange of the elements between air, earth, water, plants and animals, and these recycling processes ensure that all living things are able to live and grow.

One of the most important elements is oxygen, which exists freely as a gas in the atmosphere (21%), and is also an essential part of both the water and carbon cycles. Carbon itself and nitrogen are also vital. Others of importance include the minerals phosphorus, sulphur and calcium, and trace elements, like iron and zinc, that are needed in smaller quantities. These are all needed to supply energy for life, and are also important in the process of growth and constant renewal of all living cells.

The water cycle

Water is an essential of life, making up almost 75% of all living things. It is continuously recycled between sea, air and land, creating the conditions in which life can exist.

Clouds meet cold air, e.g. above mountains. Large drops of water form and fall as rain or snow.

Make your own water cycle

Using a large plastic bowl, a small container and some plastic wrap, you can make a miniature water cycle. Leave the bowl in the sun, with some water in it. The heat evaporates the water, which rises and condenses on the cool plastic to fall into the container.

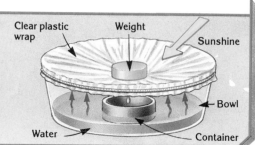

Clear plastic wrap · Weight · Sunshine · Bowl · Water · Container

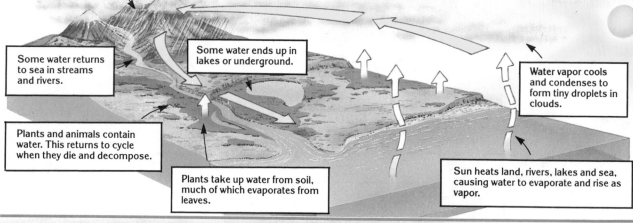

Some water returns to sea in streams and rivers.

Some water ends up in lakes or underground.

Water vapor cools and condenses to form tiny droplets in clouds.

Plants and animals contain water. This returns to cycle when they die and decompose.

Plants take up water from soil, much of which evaporates from leaves.

Sun heats land, rivers, lakes and sea, causing water to evaporate and rise as vapor.

The carbon cycle

Carbon is constantly circulating in many different forms through living things, the soil and the atmosphere.

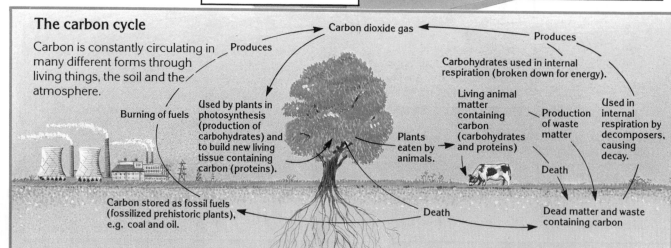

Carbon dioxide gas

Produces

Produces

Carbohydrates used in internal respiration (broken down for energy).

Burning of fuels

Used by plants in photosynthesis (production of carbohydrates) and to build new living tissue containing carbon (proteins).

Plants eaten by animals.

Living animal matter containing carbon (carbohydrates and proteins)

Production of waste matter

Used in internal respiration by decomposers, causing decay.

Death

Carbon stored as fossil fuels (fossilized prehistoric plants), e.g. coal and oil.

Death

Dead matter and waste containing carbon

The greenhouse effect

Carbon dioxide in the atmosphere plays an important role in warming the earth by trapping the sun's heat, in what is called the greenhouse effect. Since industrialization, the burning of fossil fuels has greatly increased the amount of carbon dioxide in the atmosphere.

The future effects of this build-up on global temperatures can only be guessed at. Some experts predict that temperatures will rise, melting the polar ice packs, raising sea levels to flood coastal areas, and resulting in large-scale changes in climate and agriculture around the world.

To keep the level of carbon dioxide from rising further we must increase our use of renewable energy sources and become more energy-efficient (see page 33).

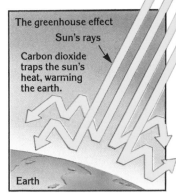

The greenhouse effect
Sun's rays
Carbon dioxide traps the sun's heat, warming the earth.
Earth

The nitrogen cycle

All living things need nitrogen to build proteins for growth. The way they get this is quite complex.

Although about 78% of air is made up of the gas nitrogen, it cannot be used by plants and animals in gaseous form. It must first be converted into nitrites and then nitrates before it can be used.

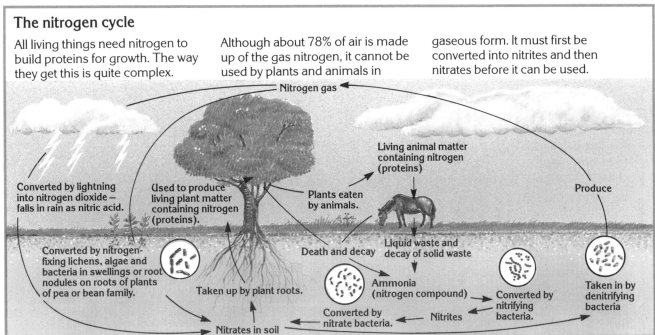

Nitrogen gas

Converted by lightning into nitrogen dioxide — falls in rain as nitric acid.

Used to produce living plant matter containing nitrogen (proteins).

Living animal matter containing nitrogen (proteins)

Plants eaten by animals.

Produce

Converted by nitrogen-fixing lichens, algae and bacteria in swellings or root nodules on roots of plants of pea or bean family.

Taken up by plant roots.

Death and decay

Liquid waste and decay of solid waste

Taken in by denitrifying bacteria

Ammonia (nitrogen compound)

Converted by nitrifying bacteria.

Converted by nitrate bacteria.

Nitrites

Nitrates in soil

The mineral cycle

Minerals originate from the earth itself, either from the surface or from deeper down through volcanic activity. Many of these, like phosphorus and iron, are needed for the life processes of plants and animals.

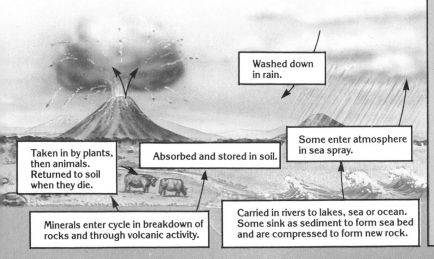

Washed down in rain.

Some enter atmosphere in sea spray.

Taken in by plants, then animals. Returned to soil when they die.

Absorbed and stored in soil.

Minerals enter cycle in breakdown of rocks and through volcanic activity.

Carried in rivers to lakes, sea or ocean. Some sink as sediment to form sea bed and are compressed to form new rock.

The natural balance

Nature's cycles are relatively stable. Any changes that do occur take place within certain limits, so that, despite minor variations, the cycles continue and life goes on. However, man's activities are fundamentally changing the environment and disturbing these natural cycles. We are upsetting the fine balance of nature, and the results may turn out to be disastrous.

Upsetting the natural balance

Disturbing the cycles

Nature's cycles form a balance in the natural world in which there is no waste. Everything is broken down and re-used. Man, however, is now creating an imbalance by creating waste and polluting the environment. Pollution occurs on different levels: personal, national and global.

Pollution

Ever since people first gathered together in settlements there has been pollution. This describes everything produced by man that does not decompose (is not **biodegradable**) and so does not return into the natural cycles. It also describes our disturbance of these cycles by producing more or less of a natural substance and so upsetting the balance.

Some pollution just looks bad, whilst other forms, like some chemical and nuclear wastes, are deadly. When population was low and there was little industry, a small amount of pollution did not really matter. Nowadays, things are very different.

An early rubbish tip
A modern tip

Recycling waste

Unlike nature, modern man produces vast amounts of waste. The average family of four in an industrialized country throws away over a ton of garbage a year, most of which ends up buried below ground. But how much of this actually is garbage.

Step 1

Study the contents of your garbage can to see what you are throwing away (do it outside on newspaper). Weigh the contents and separate them, putting them into different containers, e.g. glass, food waste, plastics, textiles, paper and metals.

You should have your parents' permission (or help) before doing this.

Wear a pair of washing-up gloves and overalls or old clothes.

Never taste or inhale unknown substances.

Be very careful of broken glass and the sharp edges of tin cans.

Step 2

Now see how much can be returned into nature's cycles or recycled for human use. Here are a few examples of how this can be done – for more ideas, contact your local environmental or conservation group (see pages 44-45).

Glass. There may well be a glass-recycling scheme in your area, in which you take your bottles and jars to bottle-banks. Ask your local authority about this. Or you can invent ways of re-using jars and bottles, e.g. as containers or vases.

Using a bottle bank

Paper. Many charities and organizations collect bundles of old newspapers and magazines to be recycled. Contact those in your area, e.g. an old people's home, to see if you and your friends can help. To make your own recycled paper, see pages 42-43.

Aluminum cans. These can be washed, crushed (stand on them) and taken to a can recycling center (look in the phone book). You may be paid for them. You could collect more at concerts, fairs, fetes, etc.

Only aluminum cans can be recycled. Use a magnet to check.

Aluminum cans are not magnetic, other cans are.

Organic waste. This is anything that will rot. It can be used as compost (see page 38).

Step 3

What is left, like plastics and chemicals, cannot at the moment be recycled. Weigh this waste – the less there is the better. See if you can decrease your family's waste, e.g. by buying products with less packaging, or by always taking the same bag to the shops with you.

Acid rain

One of the nastiest forms of pollution that we are creating today is known as acid rain. This occurs when wastes from burning fossil fuels interfere with the natural water cycle. Its effects include dying forests, lifeless lakes, damaged buildings and harm to people. We have the technology to prevent this happening, e.g. filters for power stations and catalytic converters to clean fumes from vehicle exhaust pipes. Some countries have already begun using such measures in an attempt to stop acid rain. Others have been much slower to see that action is now vital.

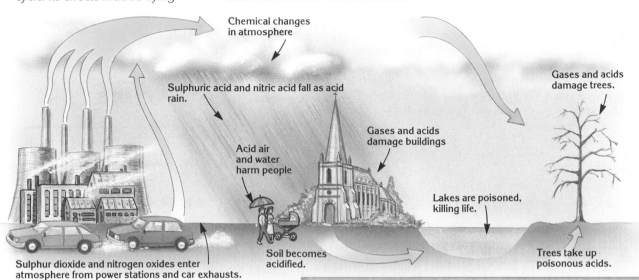

Chemical changes in atmosphere

Sulphuric acid and nitric acid fall as acid rain.

Acid air and water harm people

Gases and acids damage buildings

Gases and acids damage trees.

Lakes are poisoned, killing life.

Soil becomes acidified.

Trees take up poisonous acids.

Sulphur dioxide and nitrogen oxides enter atmosphere from power stations and car exhausts.

Chemicals in farming

In today's intensive farming the natural nitrogen and mineral cycles are neglected. Very little natural organic waste is returned to the soil, resulting in reduced levels of minerals and humus, and lower productivity. To make up for this, farmers add chemical fertilizers to the soil. These often cause environmental and health damage, e.g. when washed into rivers and lakes, eventually ending up in drinking water.

Intensive farming in Montana, USA

Many powerful chemicals are also used to fight pests, weeds and diseases in order to keep productivity high. These pesticides, herbicides and fungicides have long-lasting and damaging effects on food webs wherever they are used. The chemicals often remain on the plants which have been sprayed, and can damage human health when these are eaten.

Organic farming

Fuel shortages, increasing costs and environmental damage mean the long-term future of intensive farming is in doubt. We need to return to more natural farming methods, which work with nature's cycles. These methods are based on ecological principles and are known as organic farming.

Organic farming techniques, like crop rotation and the use of manure as fertilizer, are today being used successfully. They improve rather than endanger the environment by returning most organic waste to the soil, increasing humus and mineral levels and allowing nature's cycles to work.

Some crops use up the nitrates in the soil and others (beans and peas) restore them (see page 13). By changing the crop grown in a field each year in a rota system, the natural cycles can be used to improve growth.

Wheat

Mixed grass and clover

Turnips

Barley

Ecologists think that these techniques should be widely adopted. Many people now prefer to eat "organic" food, knowing that it is free of chemicals and has been produced without damaging the environment.

Adaptation

All living things must adapt to their environment if they are going to survive. Adaptation is the result of long-term interaction with the environment and has enabled life to spread to every part of the world. It includes changes in both behavior and physical features.

Hot deserts

Some of the best examples of adaptation occur in the world's deserts (large areas with extremely harsh environments). In hot, dry desert climates, plants and animals have developed various different survival techniques, e.g. many have physical adaptations to store water or food, or to lose heat more rapidly.

The Australian outback is the largest area of sandy desert outside the Sahara. It is made up of different types of desert, varying due to differences in climate and rock formation. The first inhabitants of the land, the Aborigines, developed a lifestyle over many thousands of years which enabled them to live in both grassland and desert. Until very recently, groups still wandered the outback, hunting and gathering food in their traditional ways.

An Australian desert

Mulga trees — they have expanded leaf stalks instead of leaves to lessen water loss by evaporation.

Marsupial mice — they avoid the day's heat in burrows and search for food at night. Their tails store fat reserves in case of food shortages.

Saltbush plants — their vast root systems collect what little water there is.

There are many other examples of adaptations to life in hot deserts. Cacti, for example, have developed spines instead of leaves to prevent water loss, and the North American jack rabbit has developed very large ears (see picture).

North American jack rabbit

The long ears contain many blood vessels near the surface, which radiate away the body's heat.

Growing a cactus garden

A shallow clay container filled with sandy soil and decorated with some stones or wood is all you need as a basis for your cactus garden. To obtain your cacti either buy them or take cuttings from someone else's plants. To do this, break off the shoots growing at the base of the parent cactus. Let them dry for a few days before putting them in the soil. Once established, cacti need a lot of sun but very little watering or attention.

A cactus garden

If you dribble water onto cacti, it will roll off. Their "skin" does not allow water to be lost, so it can't get in either.

Hedge cactus (Cereus)

Old man cactus (Cephalocereus)

Fig cactus (Opuntia)

Golden ball (Echinocactus)

Desertification

This is when dry, marginal land is turned into desert due to human activities like over-grazing or cutting down trees. Much of the earth's land surface is now threatened. The costs of preventing this and improving the damaged lands are low when compared to the gains in agricultural production once the lands are developed. But at present very little is being done and many traditional farmers, with little land or stock, are suffering badly.

The Sahel, Africa: early 1970s

Drought and desertification changed marginal land (land that is difficult to cultivate) into desert.

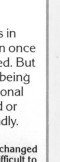

Over 100,000 people and millions of animals died.

Icy deserts

Conditions in the freezing, icy deserts of the polar regions are just as harsh as in their hot, dry equivalents. In winter, ice and snow cover the vast continent of Antarctica and its surrounding seas, as well as the entire Arctic region (see below). But living things can still be found, adapted to life in these extreme environments.

Polar bears survive the winter by hibernating in dens hollowed out under the ice. They also have large, furry feet to act as snowshoes.

Arctic fox — the color of its coat changes to fit the season: pure white in winter, browny-red in summer. This is an example of camouflage (see below).

To survive the cold, all the large animals are warm-blooded, that is, able to keep their body temperature constant despite external conditions. Thick, insulating layers of fat or fur, or both, keep the heat in and the cold out.

Huskies curl into balls to conserve heat and are protected by their thick coats of fur.

The native Eskimo people face the cold by smearing themselves with animal fat and wearing thick furs.

The Arctic summer

In the brief summers much of the ice and snow melts, revealing the Arctic tundra, which, for a while, supports a great variety of plant and animal life. The plants survive the long winter either as seeds or by not freezing (many contain "anti-freeze"), and grow and produce seeds in the short summer. Hot, dry deserts, too, have short periods when life is plentiful. These occur after rain, when water brings life to dormant seeds.

Tundra in summertime

Desert plants are ephemeral (short-lived), making the most of a very short growing season.

Arctic poppy

Camouflage and mimicry

Camouflage is the adaptation of a plant or animal to blend in with its natural surroundings so as not to be seen. This adaptation has developed to help plants and animals hide from predators. But it is also used by predators themselves to remain unseen by unsuspecting prey. Mimicry is a camouflage technique, by which animals have adapted to look like, or mimic, something else, so as to benefit in a particular way.

Plaice — uses its dull, sandy coloration to hide from predators on the sea floor.

Bee-orchid — its flower looks like a bee. This attracts bees looking for a mate, which then pollinate the plant.

A seed study

Not only do plants adapt to the environment around them, but their seeds do, too, giving them a greater chance to survive. In many cases, they are adapted for wind dispersal. Collect as many different seeds as you can find and compare the variety of shapes and sizes. Take them outside, throw them into the air and study how, and how far, they travel.

Seed adaptations

Feathery seeds, e.g. dandelion

Helicopter seeds, e.g. maple or sycamore

Explosive fruits (launch seed away from plant), e.g. gorse

Seed in edible fruit (dispersed in droppings of animal that eats it), e.g. bramble

Coniferous and deciduous forests

Coniferous and deciduous forests are two of the three major types of forest (see also tropical rainforest, pages 26-27). Life in the two areas has developed very differently, due to the differences in climate, as the examples on these pages show.

Man and the forests

Man's influence on the world's forests is wide-ranging. Forestry is very important to the economies of many countries, supplying wood to the paper, building and furniture industries, but it can often be ecologically damaging.

This is especially true when plantation trees of different, fast-growing species are planted to replace native trees – destroying wildlife habitats, endangering species, and ruining landscapes.

A coniferous plantation

Plantations are important sources of wood, but can be ecologically damaging.

Very little of the great deciduous and mixed forests of the past survive today, due to the spread of farming and urban developments.

Man's destructive activities, like the production of acid rain (see page 15), now threaten those that remain. We must realize the dangers and act now to protect these trees. To find out how to choose, plant and care for a tree, see pages 40-41.

Coniferous forests

Conifers are so called because their seeds are produced in cones. Vast coniferous forests of spruce, cedar, larch, pine and fir are found where conditions are cold and harsh, with brief summers and low rainfall, i.e. northern parts of America, Europe and Asia and in the world's mountainous areas. Further south, conifers exist alongside deciduous trees in mixed forests.

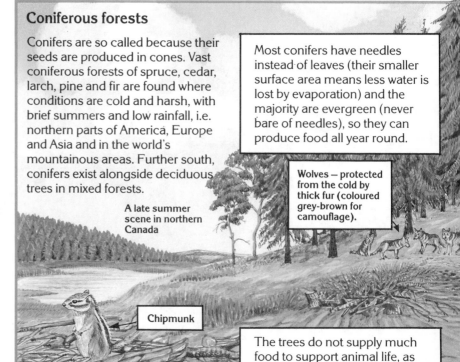

A late summer scene in northern Canada

Most conifers have needles instead of leaves (their smaller surface area means less water is lost by evaporation) and the majority are evergreen (never bare of needles), so they can produce food all year round.

Wolves – protected from the cold by thick fur (coloured grey-brown for camouflage).

Chipmunk

The trees do not supply much food to support animal life, as their needles are tough and their branches sparse.

Deciduous forests

The word deciduous describes trees that shed their leaves once a year. They are flowering plants, mainly blooming once a year in the spring. Deciduous forests are found in areas with relatively mild temperatures and plenty of rainfall throughout the year. Most of Europe, Japan, eastern Asia and the eastern USA were once covered in forests of deciduous trees, like oak, beech, maple and ash.

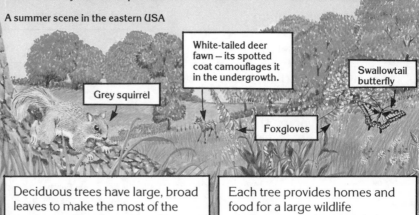

A summer scene in the eastern USA

White-tailed deer fawn – its spotted coat camouflages it in the undergrowth.

Swallowtail butterfly

Grey squirrel

Foxgloves

Deciduous trees have large, broad leaves to make the most of the many months of sunshine for photosynthesis. They are lost before winter when strong winds and cold would damage them.

Each tree provides homes and food for a large wildlife community. Rich soil and plenty of sunshine allow many different plants to flourish. These support still more animal life.

Canada geese

Red crossbill – its strong beak is specially adapted to get seeds out of cones.

Moose

Douglas fir

Identifying conifers

The shape of a conifer's needles will tell you which group of trees it belongs to. These are the major groups:

Larches: clusters of 12-20 short needles, fall in autumn.

Pines: two or more needles, joined at base.

Firs: individual needles with blunt tips.

Spruces: pointed, stiff and four-sided needles.

Cedars and junipers: small, flat, scale-shaped leaves.

Yews: flattened, leathery needles.

There are few plants at ground level because of poor soil and lack of sunlight (blocked out by the conifers). This limits animal life throughout the forest.

It is too cold for most bacteria and earthworms, so decomposition of plant matter is slow, the soil remains in undisturbed layers and there is little humus. This results in less effective nitrogen and mineral cycles.

Some animals have adapted to life in the forest all year round, e.g. moose wander far to find food, and bears and chipmunks hibernate in winter, living off fat stored from summer food.

The brief warm summer sees much more activity. Insects multiply rapidly, supplying food, e.g. for birds flocking north to nest. The conifers grow fast to make the most of the extra sun.

Acorn woodpecker – its feet and tail are adapted to allow it to grip to tree trunks.

Oak tree

Maple tree

Birch tree

Ferns and grasses

Yellow warbler

Pigmy shrew

Measuring tree heights

Pin a strip of paper to the tree at your height and measure this (in inches). Walk away from the tree, holding a ruler at arms length, until the strip is level with the 1 in mark (see picture). Note where the tree-top reaches on the in scale and multiply by your height (e.g. 10 in times 57 in = 570 or 47 ½ ft).

Your view from the right distance

Read off in scale here.

Large ruler

Mark on tree is at 1 in mark on ruler.

0 in on ruler should be level with bottom of tree.

A yearly fall of leaves and an abundance of decomposers create a soil which is rich in humus, nitrates and minerals.

Animal activity in winter is greater than in coniferous forests, but life is still more plentiful in the warm, sunny conditions of spring and summer. Plant life, insects, birds and mammals are abundant.

In southern Europe, the south-west USA, Australia, New Zealand and southern South America, many deciduous trees have adapted to very hot, dry summers by adopting coniferous features. They are evergreen, with smaller, thicker leaves to save water.

Relationships in nature

In the natural world, many of the relationships between living things (organisms) are to do with eating or being eaten, but there are just as many in which organisms work together, often to the advantage of those involved. There are many different ways in which this happens, some simple, others complex; some examples are given on these pages.

Living together

Many plants and animals live with others of the same species in groups of differing sizes, with different degrees of interaction. Small numbers of animals living together are known as social groups. Larger gatherings are known as colonies.

Lions, for example, live in small social groups called prides, in which the females do the hunting as well as caring for the young. In many social groups, however, there is a more equal sharing of the work, e.g. African meerkats (small desert mammals) take turns to look after the group's offspring. The large apes come closest to our own social grouping, with the young brought up in a family framework.

A group of rare mountain gorillas — inhabitants of the upper reaches of the rainforests of Zaire.

Colonies

Different colonial animals show different levels of social behavior, and the degree of dependence between individuals differs greatly. Many seabirds, like gannets and penguins, only form colonies out of mutual self-interest (for safety in numbers).

A colony of cormorants

Seabird colonies can be enormous — one Peruvian island was at one point home to about 5 million cormorants.

Other creatures, however, like ants, termites and bees, live together in far more complex colonies, with groups of related individuals playing specific roles (examples are given in "keeping an ant colony", above right). They depend on each other for the smooth running and continuation of the colony.

Keeping an ant colony

Ants are easy to keep and fascinating to watch. To see how to make an ant observatory, properly called a formicarium, like the one illustrated, turn to page 36. You can watch the ants at work within it and study their social behavior withot disturbing them too much.

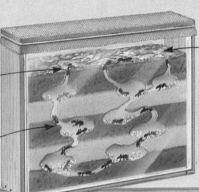

An ant observatory

Look for ants playing different roles: guarding the colony, finding food, tending the young, and looking after the queen.

Watch the ants construct a complex system of passageways and chambers.

Study which foods the ants prefer, by leaving them different sorts.

Study the different stages of their life cycle and the role of the queen.

Super-organisms

The word super-organism describes the closest form of colonial relationship, in which single organisms work together so closely that they effectively form a larger structure with its own, self-contained existence.

Coral is an example of this. Thousands of tiny animals called polyps combine to form a much larger coral structure. These polyps are interconnected by a network of links through which food can be shared.

Another example is the Portuguese man-of-war. This is not in fact a jellyfish, but a colony of many specialized polyps, each fulfilling a specific task. The resulting super-organism is a more effective life-form than the individual animals it is made up of.

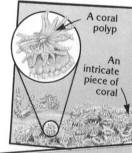

A coral polyp

An intricate piece of coral

A Portuguese man-of-war

Symbiosis

Symbiosis describes the very close relationship between two organisms of different species that live together and gain from their interaction. One common example of this is lichen, which is found on stone and wood surfaces. The main part of a lichen's body is a fungus, within which live one or more tiny, single-celled plants called algae. Both benefit greatly from their mutual arrangement (see right).

A lichen

The fungus gives the algae protection and retains a store of water.

The algae use the water and make food for themselves and the fungus by photosynthesis.

Here are two more examples of symbiosis:

In Africa ox-peckers eat insects that irritate antelope.

They also give warning of danger by flying up noisily.

This large fish allows the smaller fish to feed on parasites that live in its mouth.

Commensalism

Literally "eating at the same table", commensalism describes a relationship (less close than in symbiosis) between two organisms of different species in which food is involved. In most cases, one partner takes advantage of the feeding habits of another and gives little or nothing in return. The relationship between the house mouse and humans is a good example of commensalism.

The mouse takes advantage of food left around the house.

Humans gain nothing from the relationship.

Co-operation

There are many other forms of co-operation between living things in nature, in which both participants benefit in some way, like plants needing insects for pollination and so attracting them with nectar.

Parasites

Not all close relationships are beneficial. A parasite is a plant or animal that lives on or in another organism (the host), taking food from it whilst giving nothing or actually harming it in return. A parasite will rarely kill its host, though, as this would result in its own death, too. Lice and fleas are common parasites. Humans are often hosts to these and many others, like tapeworm and roundworm, and they also suffer from diseases, like malaria, carried by parasites.

Tapeworms up to two metres long can sometimes be found in the human intestine.

Investigating plant galls

Plant galls are home to the larvae of various insects, which are parasitic on certain trees. The adults lay their eggs inside a leaf or bud, which reacts to this intrusion by forming a growth around them. The egg turns into the larva within the gall, later emerging as an adult insect.

Plant galls can be found on many plants and trees (especially oak, birch and willow) in spring and early summer. Go out and collect some, bringing back the leaves they are on. Place them in a jar with holes in its lid, keeping this outside, and watch for the adult insect to emerge.

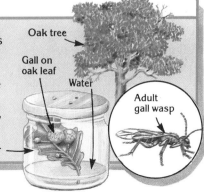

Oak tree

Gall on oak leaf

Water

Adult gall wasp

Glass jar

Population and conservation

In the natural world there is a fragile balance in plant and animal populations. There are several ways that their numbers are naturally kept in check, some of which are dealt with on this page. However, this is no longer true of the human population, the growth of which is fast destroying nature's balance, with alarming consequences for our planet.

Population control

A relatively stable balance of numbers is maintained in the wild through competition and co-existence. Predator/prey relationships and territorial behavior are the main reasons of achieving this, and these are well illustrated by the wildlife of the African savannah (see below).

Territorial behavior

All living things need food, shelter and living space. As a means of gaining these, many animals behave territorially – that is, they live (as individuals or as a social group) in a defined space, or territory, which is large enough to cater for their needs. This territory is defended against others of the same species, with the result that the overall population is kept down.

The niche

The role of an animal in its community, including what it eats, where it lives and its position in the food chain is known as its ecological niche. Different species cannot live in the same niche – they compete for resources and living space until one is forced out. Sometimes it appears that two animals share the same niche, but a closer look will show that they inhabit separate, though overlapping, ones.

Elephants feed on tall grass, while buffalo eat the young shoots and antelope graze on the short grass that is left – each occupies a different niche.

African buffalo – each herd keeps to a territory several miles wide.

Predators

Predators are animals that catch and eat other animals. They play a vital role in every ecosystem, by keeping down the population of herbivores and smaller predators on which they feed.

A pride of lions – feed on the many grazing animals, like zebra and wildebeest. Each pride has a territory of up to 5 miles across.

Feeding birds

Bird feeders or a bird table will encourage a variety of bird life into your garden or to your windowsill. Watch their different feeding preferences and techniques to work out the different niches they occupy. For details on how to make a bird table, see page 39.

Experiment with various types of food, like nuts, seeds or meat, to see what different birds prefer.

Feeding the birds throughout the winter could keep them alive.

Experiment with different feeders, like hanging bags of nuts or half a coconut, to see the birds' different feeding techniques.

Watching predators

Try to study the predators that can be found around you. Watch the domestic cat stalking its prey – it often demonstrates the hunting techniques of its much larger African relatives. Other common predators worth studying are the birds of prey (known as raptors), like hawks and kestrels.

A kestrel watching its prey (small mammals).

Smaller birds of prey often hunt beside roads and in open country.

The population problem

The world's human population is now over five billion and is rising rapidly (for more on the population problem, see page 32). This sheer weight of numbers, combined with the growing destruction caused by man, is putting great pressure on the world's wildlife and habitats. It is estimated that one plant or animal species becomes extinct every half an hour, while once common natural habitats are rapidly disappearing.

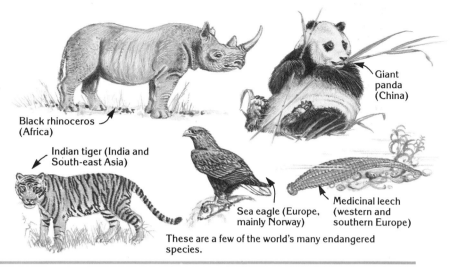

Black rhinoceros (Africa)

Indian tiger (India and South-east Asia)

Giant panda (China)

Sea eagle (Europe, mainly Norway)

Medicinal leech (western and southern Europe)

These are a few of the world's many endangered species.

Threatened habitats and wildlife

Urban expansion and the spread of intensive industry, agriculture and forestry are resulting in the destruction of important natural habitats. When these disappear, so do the many wild plants and animals that depend on them. For example, vital marine habitats, like saltmarshes and mangroves, are being polluted and destroyed at an alarming rate.

Mangrove swamp

Result of mangrove destruction

Man's greed for exotic luxuries, like fur coats and ivory jewelry, has meant that millions of animals are killed every year. As well as this, many more are caught to supply zoos, the pet trade and industrial and medical research centers. Many animals, like the cheetah and the polar bear, are now seriously endangered. This world-wide trade in wild animals is often illegal and always causes great suffering.

The need for conservation

Protection, or conservation, of wildlife and habitats is now more important than ever. The international agreements we have at present are too often ignored. We need to protect endangered species and habitats much more carefully. But in the end, it is only by becoming more aware of how we all affect the earth's environment that we will be able to safeguard the natural world.

The giant panda is the emblem of the World Wide Fund for Nature (formerly the World Wildlife Fund).

Since 1961, they have campaigned to protect the world's habitats and wildlife.

For more on what they and other organizations are doing, see pages 44-45.

Helping endangered wildlife

In every country of the world there are endangered plants and animals. Find out what is threatened in yours by contacting conservation or environmental groups (see pages 44-45). You could help them in their campaigns to help these species, or you could perhaps start your own group (see pages 42-43) to make local people more aware of the problems.

Another way to help these species is to protect or create the habitats that they prefer. Building a pond (see pages 5 and 36-37) and creating a pocket park (see pages 25 and 42-43) are two ways of doing this. Meadows, too, are easy to create, and are vital habitats for many

insects and rare wild flowers. If you have a garden, just leave an area of grass uncut and it will naturally develop into a meadow. If you live near a park, try to get the authorities to set aside an area as a meadow nature reserve.

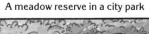

A meadow reserve in a city park

Urban ecosystems

Surprising as it may seem, large towns and cities contain a great deal of wildlife. Wherever plants and animals can find suitable conditions, including enough food, warmth and shelter, they will move in. Many have adapted their ways to life amongst people in an urban environment.

Urban adaptations

The growth of towns and cities has produced similar urban environments all over the world. In different places, different animals have adapted to fill similar niches. For instance, the brush-tailed opossum, the raccoon and the red fox play the same kind of role in urban environments on their different continents. All originally lived in open woodland, but they adapted to farmland and urban areas when these took its place.

The brush-tailed opossum and the raccoon often live in the roof spaces of suburban houses, whilst the fox makes its den in parks and areas of wasteland. All three often scavenge in dustbins for scraps of food. Their ability to adapt to different habitats and their varied diet have enabled them to live successfully in man-made environments.

Brush-tailed opossum (Australia and New Zealand)

Red fox (Europe and North America; also spreading in Australia, where it was introduced to allow the British colonists to fox hunt)

Raccoon (North America)

One bird that is found only in man-made environments is the house sparrow. Originally feeding on grain, its diet is now far more varied. This, and its ability to nest on houses and other buildings, enables it to thrive in towns and cities.

House sparrow – spread across the world in the wake of the European colonizers.

Now common in Europe, North and South America, South Africa, Australia and New Zealand.

Succession

Wherever there is an area of abandoned land, it will not be long before nature moves in. Over a period of time, a variety of plants and animals will replace each other in a process called **succession**. Mosses and grasses will usually be the first arrivals, followed by flowering plants. These attract insects, which bring birds and other wild animals. If the land is left long enough, larger plants and trees will grow. See page 28 for more about succession.

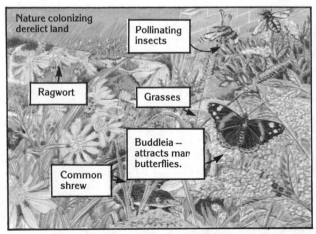

Nature colonizing derelict land

Pollinating insects

Ragwort

Grasses

Buddleia – attracts man butterflies.

Common shrew

City safari

You do not have to be in a tropical jungle or on an African plain to go on safari – a wildlife expedition around town can be just as rewarding. Study the plants and animals in those areas of your town or city that are slightly off the beaten track: wasteland, cemeteries, the wilder parts of the park and the riverbanks and canals. All you need for a satisfying safari is good observation, and perhaps a little patience. You could take your friends and make it a full-scale expedition.

Use a notebook for descriptions or sketches of what you see.

A good reference book is useful for identification.

Plan your safari before you set out, using a map of your town or city to find the areas which may be of most interest.

Transport and pollution

Pollution from the ever-growing volume of vehicle exhaust is making life more and more unpleasant in many of the world's major cities. The air contains many harmful gases like ozone, which is formed when nitrogen oxides from the exhaust react in sunlight with oxygen. Ozone, carbon monoxide, hydrocarbons and lead and dust particles all endanger the health of the cities' people and wildlife.

The removal of lead from petrol and the use of devices known as three-way catalytic converters to control exhaust fumes are two ways of lessening the problem. A long term solution, however, will only come from radical changes in

In Tokyo, Japan, special electronic signs show the levels of noise and air pollution.

transport policy and city planning. A greater emphasis on improved rail systems and public transport, combined with methods of "traffic calming", will help achieve this.

A lichen pollution test

Plants called lichens are sensitive to air pollution, especially the air's acidity (see acid rain, page 15), so you can use their presence or absence to see how clean your air is. Shrubby and leafy lichens only survive in clean air. In the most polluted areas there are none at all. Look for lichens on walls, stones and trees, and use this scale to rate the air quality.

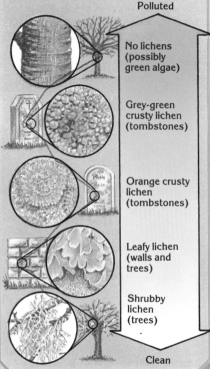

Polluted

No lichens (possibly green algae)

Grey-green crusty lichen (tombstones)

Orange crusty lichen (tombstones)

Leafy lichen (walls and trees)

Shrubby lichen (trees)

Clean

An example of "traffic calming"

The aim is to create a better sense of community, safer roads and a pleasanter environment.

Pedestrians and cyclists are better catered for, with wider pavements and cycle paths.

Bends, bollards and road humps keep vehicle speed down.

The streets are made more attractive with trees, flowerbeds and benches.

Creating a pocket park

Creating a miniature nature reserve, or pocket park, on derelict ground or wasteland is quite a task and probably calls for a team effort. The aim is to create a complete ecosystem in miniature, with perhaps a pond, areas of grassland and trees and bushes, in the heart of a town or city. It will provide pleasure for all the local people, and attract native wildlife back to the area.

There may already be a project in action in your area – ask at your local library, community centre, or contact your local conservation or environmental group. You could probably join in and help. If not, you could search for a suitable site in your area (like a piece of wasteland) and start your own project with a group of friends (for more about this, see pages 42-43).

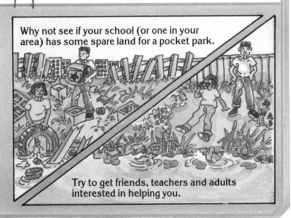

Why not see if your school (or one in your area) has some spare land for a pocket park.

Try to get friends, teachers and adults interested in helping you.

Tropical rainforests

Great rainforests stretch around the Equator, covering large parts of Central and South America, Central Africa, South-east Asia and northern Australasia. These forests are the most complex ecosystems in the world and contain a wealth of resources. Despite their importance, though, they are being destroyed at an alarming rate.

Rainforests grow in areas where rainfall and temperatures are both high and constant. Over millions of years they have developed into the earth's richest wildlife habitats. They cover less than 10% of the planet's land surface, but they contain between 50% and 70% of all plant and animal species. The greatest of all the forests is Amazonia in Brazil, featured on these pages.

Toucan – its large, strong beak helps it pick fruit from a distance and also frightens predators.

Build your own rainforest

Using a large fish-tank, you can (almost) re-create the rainforest environment in miniature. Place a layer of gravel and charcoal at the bottom, covered with about an inch of rich compost. Shape the ground with small stones under the compost. Dampen the compost and add a variety of exotic plants.
With a glass top and kept in a warm, well-lit spot, out of the sun, the plants should flourish.

The air is moist, and water is continually recycled between compost, plant, air and tank. Add a little water every few months.

A variety of exotic plants – available from plant or flower shops.

Small flowering plants, like orchids, add color.

Delicate ferns

Don't plant them too close together, as they need room to grow.

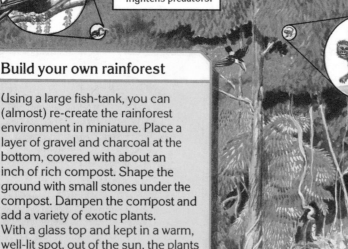

Harpy eagle

Emerald tree boa

Woolly monkey

Native Indian, hunting with blow-pipe. Brazil's Indian population has fallen from 5 million to 200,000 over the past 400 years.

Many of the largest trees have developed buttresses for support, as their roots are very shallow.

Layering

All rain forests have a similar structure, with five main layers, each with its own specific plant and animal life. These layers often merge together, or sometimes one or more are absent.

Emergent layer – made up of a few of the tallest trees which rise 30 to 50 ft above the mass of greenery below. From here, Harpy eagles and other birds of prey watch alertly for the animals on which they feed.

Canopy – 100 to 130 ft above the ground, and some 30 ft thick, this is a continuous green roof formed by the interlinking leaves and branches of the tree tops. Most of the forest's many plants and animals are found here, taking advantage of the abundant sunshine.

Understorey – made up of the tops of smaller trees that receive less light, like palms, and of younger trees struggling to reach upwards. Much sparser than the canopy, it has its own community of plant and animal life.

Shrub layer – consisting of shrubs and small trees, this layer depends on sunlight penetrating the upper layers. If none reaches here, both this and the herb layer will be sparse.

When a gap appears in the canopy, sunlight reaches the lower regions, causing the shrub and herb layers to grow rapidly.

Herb layer – ferns and herbs making up a layer of undergrowth. Elusive ground dwellers, like the tapir, live down here, along with many insects.

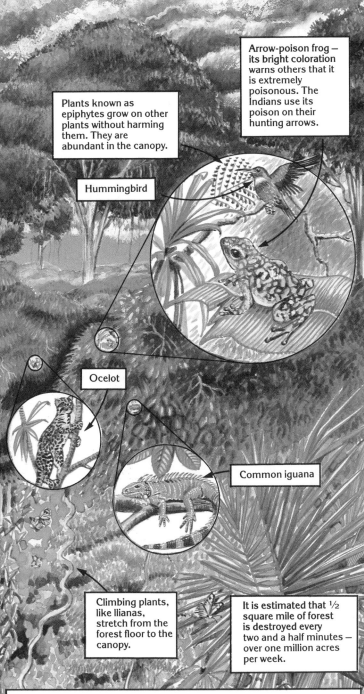

Plants known as epiphytes grow on other plants without harming them. They are abundant in the canopy.

Arrow-poison frog — its bright coloration warns others that it is extremely poisonous. The Indians use its poison on their hunting arrows.

Hummingbird

Ocelot

Common iguana

Climbing plants, like llianas, stretch from the forest floor to the canopy.

It is estimated that ½ square mile of forest is destroyed every two and a half minutes — over one million acres per week.

The forest floor is covered by several inches of fallen leaves. Here, organic matter is rapidly recycled by the decomposers, and minerals are transferred directly to shallow plant roots. This process is so efficient that the lower layer of soil has little mineral content and most of the forest's mineral wealth is stored in the vegetation.

When the forest is cleared and burned, the minerals stored in vegetation are turned to ashes. The root systems are destroyed, allowing rain to wash away the ashes and topsoil. The remaining soil soon becomes infertile, turning areas once rich in life into wasteland. It takes centuries for the forest to return, if ever.

People of the forest

The rainforest is home to many native peoples, who live in harmony with its environment. Their knowledge of the forest is very important to us, if we are to understand its workings and resources. But every day these people are being forced from their own lands with no regard to their wishes or basic human rights. Both they and their knowledge are being destroyed, along with the forests in which they live.

The importance of rainforests

Tropical rainforests play a vital role in regulating the world's climate, through their position in the oxygen, carbon and water cycles. They are the most important source of raw materials for new medicines and are a vital source of new foods (at least 1,650 rainforest plants could be used as vegetables).

We have hardly started to tap the rainforests' vast resources. However, this must be done in a sustainable way, that is, we must find a balance between making good use of the forest resources, like timber, rubber and nuts, and conserving the forests themselves.

Tapping rubber in the rain forest

Destruction of the rainforests

Almost 50% of the world's rainforests have already been destroyed, and the destruction continues. The underlying causes of this are the growing populations, poverty and unequal land distribution in countries with rainforests. This is made worse by the rich nations' demand for timber, and large, badly-planned aid programs. A long-term solution will only be found when these underlying causes are properly dealt with.

The result of forest clearance

Change in nature

Everything around us is constantly changing, from microscopic living cells to the landscapes in which we live. Some changes are rapid, others take millions of years. On these pages are examples of different sorts of change, both natural and man-made.

The changing landscape

For billions of years, great natural forces, like the earth's movement, volcanic activity, erosion and the rising and falling of oceans, have been reshaping the face of the earth and its environments. They are still doing so, but so slowly that it is hardly noticeable.

The features of Monument Valley (western USA) have been carved by erosion over millions of years.

More short-term changes in the natural world are known as **succession**. This is when a series of different plants and animals replace each other over a period of time until a **climax community** is formed. This is a community which will survive virtually unchanged if there are no disturbances in the climate, e.g. the tropical rainforests.

Succession resulting in a climax community.

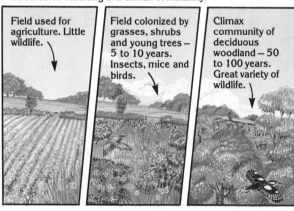

Field used for agriculture. Little wildlife.

Field colonized by grasses, shrubs and young trees – 5 to 10 years. Insects, mice and birds.

Climax community of deciduous woodland – 50 to 100 years. Great variety of wildlife.

The changes made by man to the earth's natural conditions can be seen all around us. In many places, farming, industry and urban developments have changed natural landscapes into man-made environments such as fields, towns and cities. Much of this has taken place over centuries, but increasing populations and industrialization in recent times have caused a dramatic increase in both the scale and intensity of these changes.

Changes in climate

The climate in different regions of the world changes throughout the year, according to the season. This is because the earth's axis is tilted while it travels around the sun. In tropical areas, with temperatures constant all year round, the amount of rainfall determines the season – dry or rainy. Further north and south, the climatic changes are much greater (especially in temperature), and there are four main seasons – winter, spring, summer and autumn.

The earth revolves around the sun at an angle, with its axis 23° off-center.

The angle of the sun's rays creates the difference in climate.

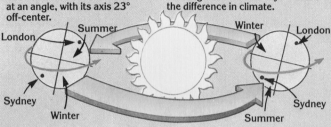

Summer in London will be winter in Sydney.

Photographing seasonal change

If you can get hold of a camera, try to take a series of photographs of the same natural scene over a period of time (perhaps the first day of each month for a year). The changes you will catch on film are fascinating. You could use them for a display, showing the variety of seasonal change.

The same scene in winter and summer

There are also more long-term climatic changes, which dramatically affect the earth's environment. Over the last 900,000 years there have been roughly ten major cold periods (ice-ages), with warmer weather between them. At present, it seems that we are in one of these warmer periods.

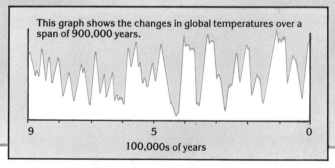

This graph shows the changes in global temperatures over a span of 900,000 years.

9   5   0

100,000s of years

Natural climatic changes take place gradually over thousands of years and so are no great threat to us at present. Of far greater importance is the danger that our large-scale industrial activity is changing the earth's climate. These changes will happen much more quickly and could well be much more dramatic. The greenhouse effect (see page 13), smoke and dust clouds blocking out sunlight, and the destruction of the ozone layer are all real threats.

Destruction of the ozone layer

High up in the atmosphere, a layer of ozone protects the earth from the sun's deadly ultra-violet rays, which cause skin cancer.

It seems that chemical compounds known as chlorofluorocarbons (CFCs), used in some aerosol cans and in making polystyrene and refrigerators, are gradually destroying this vital layer.

Some international action has already been taken to slow down the manufacture of CFCs, but many scientists want much more to be done.

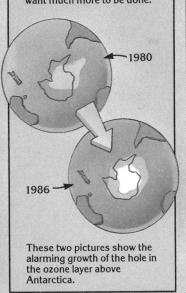

These two pictures show the alarming growth of the hole in the ozone layer above Antarctica.

Changes in living things

Everything in the living world is changing. Cells in all living things are constantly breaking down and being replaced by new ones. Individual plants and animals are produced, grow, reproduce and die – to be replaced by new generations. There are also great changes in life cycles and behaviour patterns whilst they live.

The seasonal differences in climates result in many changes in living things. Many animals adapt their life cycles to the changes in temperature and availability of food. Some **migrate** to other areas, often hundreds of miles away, where conditions are more suitable for feeding or breeding, or both.

The Arctic tern breeds in the summer on the shores of the Arctic ocean, then flies 12,500 miles to the Antarctic to feed during its summer.

It travels over 25,000 miles each year.

Many plants have adapted to seasonal changes by adjusting the times at which they produce flowers and seeds. Herbaceous perennials, for instance, die back at the end of each year, and leave just their underground stem and roots to survive the winter. Annuals survive the cold months as seeds. They flower and produce more seeds in the warmer months, dying off before winter.

Other animals, like snakes and hedgehogs, avoid the worst seasonal conditions by **hibernation**. They spend the winter months in a deep sleep, in which their body functions shut down to a minimum. Fat stored from summer feeding provides the little energy they need. **Aestivation** (or **estivation**) is like hibernation, except that it takes place where animals (like the African lungfish) need to survive very hot temperatures and drought conditions.

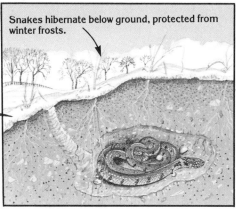

Snakes hibernate below ground, protected from winter frosts.

Daffodils are herbaceous perennials

Poppies are annuals

Watching butterfly metamorphosis

One of the most astonishing changes in the life cycles of living things is that from a caterpillar into a butterfly or moth, in a process called **metamorphosis**. To watch this, first build a container as shown in the diagram. Then find some caterpillars, placing them inside the box with a plentiful supply of the plant on which they are feeding (make sure this never runs out). At some point the caterpillars will transform themselves into pupae, from which the adult butterflies or moths will emerge. These should be let go as soon as possible.

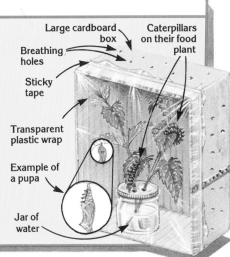

Large cardboard box

Caterpillars on their food plant

Breathing holes

Sticky tape

Transparent plastic wrap

Example of a pupa

Jar of water

Evolution

Living things have been changing and developing ever since life started around 3.5 billion years ago. This process of long-term change is known as evolution. By studying this and its link with changes in the environment, ecologists have learnt a lot about the planet's workings. They have also seen how vital the links are between living things and their environment.

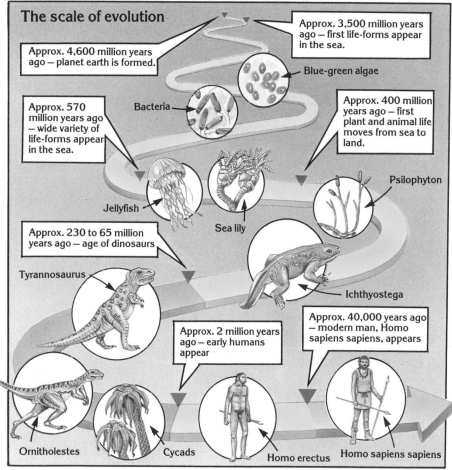

The scale of evolution

Approx. 4,600 million years ago — planet earth is formed.

Approx. 3,500 million years ago — first life-forms appear in the sea.

Blue-green algae

Bacteria

Approx. 570 million years ago — wide variety of life-forms appear in the sea.

Approx. 400 million years ago — first plant and animal life moves from sea to land.

Jellyfish

Sea lily

Psilophyton

Approx. 230 to 65 million years ago — age of dinosaurs

Tyrannosaurus

Ichthyostega

Approx. 40,000 years ago — modern man, Homo sapiens sapiens, appears

Approx. 2 million years ago — early humans appear

Ornitholestes

Cycads

Homo erectus

Homo sapiens sapiens

The development of a human embryo in the mother's womb can be seen as evidence of the process of evolution. In the nine-month period of pregnancy, it undergoes a complicated process of development, starting off as a single cell and finally being born as a complex human.

These changes mirror those that took place over billions of years, in which life evolved from tiny, single-celled organisms into the complex structures of today. At one point, the human embryo even develops tiny gill slits, showing the connection to our distant relatives of the fish world.

The development of a human embryo

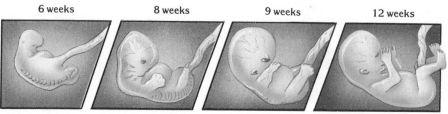

6 weeks

8 weeks

9 weeks

12 weeks

Fossils — a key to evolution

A fossil is the remains or the imprint of a plant or animal that has somehow been preserved in rock. Sometimes this happens when the shell or bone of an animal turns to mineral and thus its shape is preserved. Or the shape of the plant or animal is left imprinted in the rock, once its actual body has decayed away. The study of fossils, known as palaeontology, is one of the main ways we can find out about life in the distant past and how it has evolved.

Because they are found in specific layers of rock that can be aged, scientists can tell how old the fossils are.

By comparing fossils of different periods, we can see how life evolved.

Sometimes whole dinosaur skeletons are found fossilized.

Tools

Fossilized bones

A fossil hunter, or palaeontologist

Fossil hunting

Fossils are commonly found where sandstone, limestone or slate are exposed, though they are found elsewhere, too. All you need is a hammer and chisel and something to keep your samples in. Be observant when looking for fossils, as it is often very hard to spot the signs. Look for anything that seems out of place – different shapes, colours and types of rock. Use the hammer and chisel to break up lumps of rock to look inside. If you are successful, you could start your own fossil collection.

Here are some examples of what you may find:

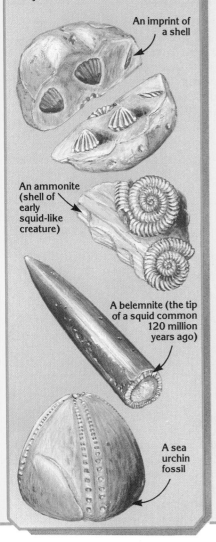

An imprint of a shell

An ammonite (shell of early squid-like creature)

A belemnite (the tip of a squid common 120 million years ago)

A sea urchin fossil

Darwinism

There are many different ideas about how the evolutionary process works. For the last 150 years, the theories of Charles Darwin have been accepted by most people as the best explanation. These depend on the idea of natural selection, or "survival of the fittest", to explain how living things have evolved into so many complex forms.

The natural selection theory states that the plants and animals that adapt best to their environment survive.

These then pass on their adaptations, which can include slight changes in physical structure, to the next generation.

In this way, living things can gradually change, or evolve, over long periods of time.

For example, smog in 19th century Britain made survival easier for dark coloured peppered moths rather than silver ones, so more passed on their characteristics and their numbers increased.

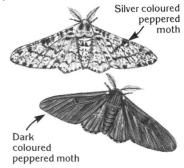

Silver coloured peppered moth

Dark coloured peppered moth

Beyond Darwinism

Some modern scientists think there are many things about evolution that Darwinism fails to explain adequately. They see natural selection as only one part of a much more complex process. Some think that evolution from simple cells into complex organisms shows that living things have an in-built tendency to organize their body structures and functions in ever more complicated ways. Whatever the truth, we are still a long way from fully understanding evolution.

The living planet

The earth itself has been changing over billions of years, too. In fact, life and the planet have constantly been evolving together, each affecting the other's development. For example, it was the early blue-green algae that, over millions of years, created the oxygen in the atmosphere, without which more complex life-forms would not have developed. Some scientists argue that the whole planet and its atmosphere works like a living organism. The idea of a "living" planet is known as the Gaia hypothesis, after the Greek Goddess of the Earth.

The planet earth seen from space – one vast living organism?

Man's responsibility

We now have the ability to create our own environments, and thus to control, to an extent, our future evolution. We also control the future of the earth and all that it supports. However, we are only just beginning to realize what a huge responsibility this is. There are many choices to be made and there is much to be done – some of our options are discussed in the following four pages.

People and planet

The human population is increasing at such a rate that both the environment and the balance of nature are threatened. This is one of the world's most urgent problems. But there are no simple answers, because it is the result of wide-ranging social, economic and political conditions which are all interconnected and which must be dealt with as a whole.

Population growth

It took thousands of years for the world's population to reach 1 billion*, sometime in the 1830s, but only another 100 years for the 2 billion mark to be reached in the 1930s. By 1975 the population had reached 4 billion and 12 years later it had grown by another billion, reaching 5 billion towards the end of 1987. It is thought that it will finally level out at about 10 billion towards the end of the next century.

This graph shows the growth, and predicted growth, of the world's population.

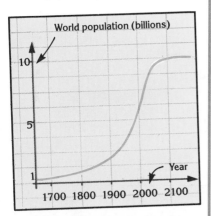

Most of this growth is taking place in the world's poorest countries, where the birth rate is greater than the death rate.

Population and resources

The earth has enough resources to support its population of 5 billion and more. But at present this is not happening. Millions of people in the poor world are living in hunger and poverty. The population problem is not so much "too many people" or "not enough land", as not managing to properly feed and support the growing populations.

Population problems do not necessarily come from a shortage of land:

Holland has a high population density but no problem, because it can afford to feed its population. India and Brazil have more land per person, but have a problem because they are poor.

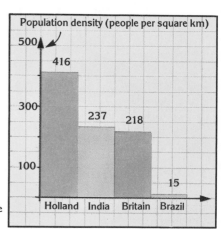

A major part of the problem is the unequal sharing of the earth's resources between the rich and poor nations, and between the rich and poor people within those nations. The average American born today, for example, will use 40 times as much of the earth's resources (e.g. food, fossil fuels, metals, etc.) as their equivalent in a poor African country. One cause of this is the unfair system of international trade, in which poor nations are forced to compete with each other to produce and export crops (like coffee) more and more cheaply, to the benefit of the rich nations.

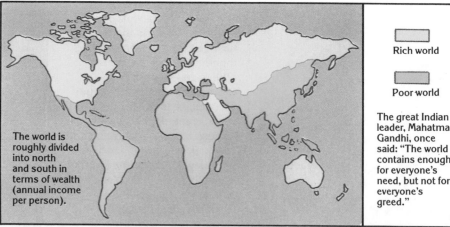

The world is roughly divided into north and south in terms of wealth (annual income per person).

Rich world

Poor world

The great Indian leader, Mahatma Gandhi, once said: "The world contains enough for everyone's need, but not for everyone's greed."

Population and the environment

Many of the world's major ecological threats, like desertification (page 16) and rainforest destruction (page 27), are not necessarily caused by growing populations. The international economy, controlled by the wealthy nations, is also partly to blame. Many poor farmers are pushed off the best land, which is then used to grow export crops for the rich countries. They are forced to use poorer land or clear forest to produce the food they need to survive. To stop the environmental damage that this causes, there need to be changes in both national and international economic policies. The rich nations are the ones who can influence these policies, and so they control the future of the poor nations and their environments.

* These figures are based on the American billion, i.e. 1,000,000,000 (in other countries, e.g. Britain, one billion = 1,000,000,000,000).

Energy and the environment

Energy is vital for many of our basic needs, like cooking, heating and transport. Its production has a big influence on the environment we live in, so we must choose carefully the sources of energy that are to be used in the future. The choices that we make now will determine what the society and environment of tomorrow will be like.

Today's energy

The wealthy nations depend mainly on fossil fuels (coal, oil and gas) to provide their energy. They also produce some by nuclear power (using radioactive uranium) and some by hydro-electric power (using falling water). But the methods used are now seriously damaging the environment, e.g. the burning of fossil fuels causes acid rain and the greenhouse effect, and nuclear power produces long-term radioactive pollution and waste (and the danger of accidents).

In poorer countries the main source of domestic energy is wood (oil is used for industrial and transport purposes). This, too, has resulted in major environmental problems, with widespread deforestation (cutting down of trees) and soil erosion.

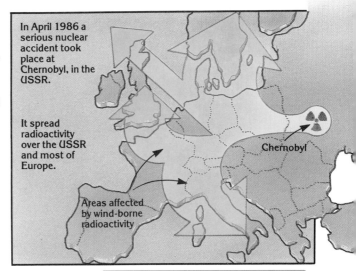

In April 1986 a serious nuclear accident took place at Chernobyl, in the USSR.

It spread radioactivity over the USSR and most of Europe.

Chernobyl

Areas affected by wind-borne radioactivity

Renewable energy

Safer and cleaner forms of energy production are now being introduced in many countries. These are known as renewable energy sources, as they will not run out, like fossil fuels eventually will. They are now being used successfully in different areas of the world and promise plenty of energy in the future, with far less risk to the environment. Below and to the right are some examples.

Wind power generator in Scotland.

● Solar power can be active (the use of solar panels to produce electricity) or passive (using more glass in buildings to trap the sun's heat) and has great potential, even in less sunny climates like those of northern Europe.

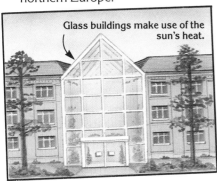

Glass buildings make use of the sun's heat.

● Wind power is now being used for large-scale electricity production. It is especially useful for supplying remote communities and small-scale users.

● The use of specially planted, fast-growing plants and trees could supply local fuel needs.

● Burning industrial waste and urban refuse in smaller, more efficient combined heat and power (CHP) stations produces energy as well as solving the refuse problem.

Other sources include converting wave and tide energy into electricity, and the tapping of geothermal energy (the heat of the earth's core). There are some environmental problems with the use of some of these sources on a large scale, but these are minor when compared to the problems and limits of fossil fuels and the dangers of more nuclear accidents.

Conserving energy

One way of lessening our use of fossil and nuclear fuels is to use energy more efficiently, so that less is actually needed. This can be done on a national scale – by saving energy used in industry and transport. But it can also be done at the level of the individual. Your actions, too, will make a difference. Here are some ideas:

Insulate your hot-water tank and pipes (as in the picture) – your water will heat up quicker and stay hot longer.

Don't waste electricity, e.g. turn off lights when not in use, have a shower or all-over wash instead of a bath (it uses less heated water).

Draftproof your doors and windows – this is simple to do and very effective.

Help your parents insulate the loft (if you have one) – this can save up to 20% of your energy bill.

The future

We are now finding ourselves faced with choices about the sort of environment that we want to live in. The main choice is whether to start working with nature, by understanding and working with its natural cycles, or to carry on working against it. The future of all the people in the world, and of the world itself, depends on the choices that we make today.

Solving the environmental crisis

Today, man's pressure on the natural world is causing a worldwide environmental crisis. Below are some of the main problems that we now face, along with some actions that we could take to improve the situation.

Soil erosion

Soil erosion occurs when the vital topsoil is removed in the wind and rain.

– reforestation (the planting of trees) – trees and hedgerows act as wind-breaks and their roots bind the soil.

– organic farming – organic matter retains water longer and binds the soil better, preventing it drying up and blowing away.

– smaller fields – the smaller the field, the more protected the soil will be.

Rainforest destruction

– reforms in land ownership in rainforest countries – to take the pressure off rainforest land.

– control of ranching and logging in rainforest areas, by lessening the rich world's demand for meat and tropical hardwoods.

– sustainable methods for using the forest's resources (methods that work with the natural cycles, and so can go on continuously), e.g. rubber-tapping.

Acid rain and other pollution

– pollution filters on power stations and motor vehicles.

– renewable energy sources.

– alternatives to artificial chemicals in farming.

– an end to pollution from industrial and nuclear sources.

Desertification

Desertification takes place when poor, arid land is over-used and turns to desert.

– less dependency on export crops in the poor world (these are grown on the best land, forcing poor people onto the more sparse land which soon turns to desert).

– appropriate irrigation techniques.

– more tree-planting schemes.

Destruction of habitats and wildlife

– more and larger wildlife parks in towns and countryside.

– stricter international controls and safeguards to protect natural habitats and prevent the killing and trading of wild animals.

Ozone depletion

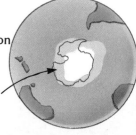

The protective ozone layer in the atmosphere is in danger of being destroyed.

– a complete ban on the production and use of chlorofluorocarbons (as soon as it is practically possible).

The greenhouse effect

– renewable energy sources.

– a halt to the destruction of the rainforest (these act as 'sinks', taking carbon dioxide from the air and using it up in photosynthesis).

– lower levels of energy use and wastage.

The wasting of our natural resources

– recycling of essential minerals.

– emphasis on building things to last and repairing them (rather than just throwing them away).

– better schemes to encourage us to change our wasteful lifestyles.

Practical action

All the suggested actions on the previous page must happen worldwide if they are to be successful. This demands much more international cooperation, especially between rich and poor nations. The trouble is that politicians tend to be more concerned with gaining support in their own countries in the short-term, than with the long-term future of the world and its people.

Many people believe that even all these actions will not be enough, and that we must all make very great changes in the way we live. They are working towards this in what is known as the green movement (see green politics, on page 45). This used to be called the ecology movement.

At the moment it is mainly charity organizations, like Oxfam, that are successfully helping the world's poor to help themselves.

They give small-scale aid to communities, solving their problems without destroying local ways and traditions.

They use appropriate technology that the users can work and maintain, like this wind-powered pump in Africa.

The sunflower is one of the images used in the green movement. It represents regrowth (of a more ecologically-sound society).

The problems are worldwide, but we can all do something to help. Every small change you make to your life will mean that the overall situation improves. This book shows you some ways you can help — if you want to do more, contact the groups listed on pages 44-45.

Genetic engineering

One major problem that we are now facing is the control of genetic engineering. This is when scientists use living organisms (or parts of them) to change or create other life forms. They often experiment with genes, the parts of cells holding the genetic "code" that determines the characteristics of an organism.

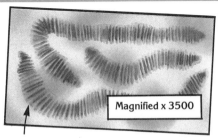

Magnified x 3500

By changing the information stored in the genes of an organism, scientists alter the characteristics of the new generation it produces.

Genetic experiments show how modern technology can be both a promise and a threat. For instance, some micro-organisms have been engineered to kill caterpillar pests, but some people feel that these organisms could seriously threaten the balance of nature. We need much stricter controls on such experiments than are now in use.

Antarctica — a test case

Antarctica is a continent almost untouched by the activities of man. However, many of the rich nations are now showing a keen interest in it, as it may hold huge reserves of oil and minerals. Other, poorer countries are also demanding a share. Environmental groups, like Greenpeace, believe it should be held in trust for the future as a world park. What happens to Antarctica is a test of our ability to cooperate now, in the interests of future generations.

Antarctica has a land surface greater than that of the USA and Mexico combined.

As a world park, Antarctica would be open to all for scientific research and protected from destruction.

Any oil pollution would seriously endanger the fragile ecosystem. The low temperature would drastically slow the breakdown of oil.

The holistic view

It is now very important that we learn to respect the natural world, not just because it supplies our basic needs (like food, water and air), but because it has a right to exist on its own merits. When we see that we are a part of this natural world, and not separate and above it, we begin to see the importance of protecting the great variety of living things it is made up of.

The holistic view looks at the natural world as an interconnected whole — the web of life — rather than a collection of many different parts. If we destroy separate strands of this web, we will end up destroying the web itself. If we do that, then we destroy ourselves.

Ecology projects

On the next few pages are some larger-scale projects that you could do, either alone or with friends, parents or teachers. They are all enjoyable and will help you learn more about ecology.

Building an ant observatory

For an introduction to keeping an ant colony, see page 20. Here you can find out how to make a formicarium, or observatory, to keep the ants in.

What you will need:

3 pieces of wood (15 in long, 2 in wide and over 1 in deep)

2 pieces of perspex or plastic (15 in by 17 in)

Some strong glue (for use on plastic and wood)

6 thin nails (2 in long) and a hammer

A piece of old stocking and a strong elastic band

Some garden soil, sand and leaf litter

A colony of ants

What to do

Take the 3 pieces of wood and, using the glue and nails, fasten them together in a U-shape as shown.

Take care when using hammer and nails.

Wait until the glue dries. Then take one piece of plastic and, putting glue around the outside of the wooden frame, stick the two together. Turn it round and do the same with the second piece of plastic on the other side.

Leave this to dry for a day or two. Now fill it with alternating layers of sand and soil (so the tunnels and chambers will show), topping it off with a thin layer of leaf litter.

Leave a 5 in gap at the top, to allow the ants some space. You could put in some twigs and leaves, too.

Collect the ants (try under large stones), using a soft brush and a jar – try to include the much larger queen ant. Empty them into their new home.

Give them some water (a moist lump of cotton), and some sugar, apple or other food-scraps. Secure the stocking or tea-towel around the top with the elastic band. Now watch the ants work.

Making a pond

One way to improve your environment and help local wildlife is to build a pond. To see what it might look like when completed, turn to page 5.

What you will need:

A spade

A very large sheet of plastic

Some large stones and some hay or straw

Old carpet or rags

Pond plants (grown in baskets) and pond weed

Plenty of water (rainwater is best)

A bucket of water, weeds and mud from another pond

Positioning

If you have a garden, putting in a pond will add interest. If you don't, you could try to find some land nearby, like school grounds or parkland, and get permission to build a pond there.

Keep the pond away from trees if you can, as falling leaves can be a big problem in autumn.

It is best to place the pond near some sort of cover, like a flower bed, hedge or rockery, as this will give frogs and toads some sort of protection.

Digging the pond

When making your own pond, you are free to design its shape.

Dig a hole at least 6 ft across and 1½ ft deep.

The sides should be gently sloping, with shelves at different levels.

Remove all the stones that stick out of the bottom and sides, and cover the bottom with old carpet or rags (this will stop anything puncturing the plastic).

Laying the plastic

Wash the plastic sheet thoroughly (to get rid of any chemicals still on it). Then lay it in the hole. Don't worry if it doesn't fit the contours exactly – the weight of the water will help.

Secure the sheet with large stones around the edge of the pond. You could use paving stones for this.

Place a 4 in layer of soil over the bottom of the pond (using some of the earth that you have just dug up). This will give plants a good base to grow from.

Filling the pond

Using a hosepipe or buckets, fill the pond with water. Don't fill it right up to the top – leave 2½ to 5 in – or else it will overflow when it rains.

Add your bucket of water, weed and mud from another pond. This will be full of animals, plants and seeds and will help life establish itself in your pond much more quickly.

Place your plants in the pond. These should be indigenous (plants that grow naturally in your local area). To make it easier to arrange them, you should keep them in their in baskets. Use small stones to attach pond weed to the bottom.

Let the mud and soil in the water settle.

Place some larger stones on the bottom for shelter, and also near the edges to help animals get in and out.

Add some hay or straw at the bottom to encourage scavengers and decomposers.

You could place a dead tree branch sticking out of the water, to give birds somewhere to perch.

Keeping the pond

If the pond gets too murky, put in plenty of pond-snails. These clean the water by feeding on the tiny algae that can make it dirty.

A few leaves blown into the pond will be beneficial. They will decompose on the bottom, releasing minerals. But try to keep the pond free of too many, especially in autumn, as they will cause problems.

Larger animals, like toads, frogs and newts, will find their own way to your pond after a while. Keep an eye out for them, but be patient.

Unless you want an ornamental fish pond, don't add fish to your pond (especially if it is quite small). They are greedy predators and will eat the smaller pond life.

You may need to top up the water level in dry periods, as some water will evaporate.

Ecology projects

Building a compost heap

If you have a garden and enjoy gardening, a compost heap is a useful addition. Most soils will benefit from added compost, as it returns vital minerals that are used up in plant growth, and it is more natural than adding chemicals.

What you will need:

Organic waste from the kitchen (tea leaves, potato peelings, left-over food, etc. – but not meat scraps)

Organic matter from the garden (like cut grass, leaves and weeds)

A nitrogen "activator" (speeds up decay), like manure

Some soil

Plenty of water

Some planks (of the same length) and 4 wooden posts

A hammer and nails

A piece of old carpet or plastic sheeting

What to do

The first thing to do is to box in the site:

Find a spot for the heap – about 1½ square yards in size.

Firmly plant four corner posts. Use planks for the walls. Include gaps for ventilation.

You could use bricks, too. Make sure that it's stable and has ventilation gaps.

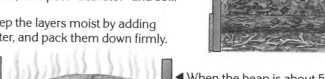

The bottom layer should be twigs and sticks. Then add alternating layers of garden waste, kitchen waste, compost "activator" and soil. ▶

Keep the layers moist by adding water, and pack them down firmly.

Take care when using a hammer and nails. Keep the nail straight and tap gently to begin with. Finish by hammering firmly.

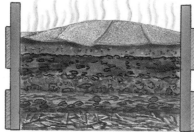

◀ When the heap is about 5 ft high lay the old carpet or plastic sheeting over the top – this keeps in the heat.

Leave it for 5 to 6 months, keeping it damp throughout this time. You could start a second heap in the meantime.

Decomposers will break down the organic matter in the heap, creating a mineral-rich compost. This can then be added to your vegetable patch, flower bed or any other soil, and will help your plants to grow.

Sprouting beans and seeds to eat

Making bean and seed sprouts is easy, fun and supplies cheap and healthy food (they are a good source of vitamin C).

What you will need:

Some large plastic containers

Some beans or seeds from a shop, e.g. mung beans, cress, chickpeas or alfalfa seeds

Some pieces of muslin or old tea-towels

Some strong elastic bands

What to do

Clean out your plastic container – you could use a large yoghurt carton, or cut the top off a large plastic soft-drinks bottle and use the main body. Put in the beans or seeds, cover them in water and leave them to soak overnight.

Attach the muslin or tea-towel over the top with the elastic band and strain out the water. Leave the container and its contents in a warm, dark place overnight. The next day, take it out, wash the beans or seeds in water, drain them and put them back again. Do this each day and check their progress.

After 3 to 4 days, they should be ready to eat. Wash them and add them to a salad or use them as a sandwich filler – they are delicious and very nutritious.

Building a bird-table

Building a bird table and providing a regular supply of food will encourage birds to your garden, and help to keep them alive in the long winter months. For more information on feeding birds, see page 22.

What you will need:

A strong wooden post about 5 ft long.

A piece of wood 20 in square and 1 in thick

A hammer, nails and 4 strips of wood 18 in long

What to do

◀ One end of the post must be shaped to a point, to go into the ground more easily. Get an adult to help you do this, or buy one with a pointed end.

Carefully nail or tack the ▶ 4 strips of wood to the outside edge of the table-top, as shown here. These will stop the food from blowing away.

Remember: take care when using hammer and nails.

There should be small gaps at each corner to allow rainwater to drain.

◀ Nail the table-top to the top of the post (you could first drill small holes in the table-top for the nails, to prevent the wood splitting).

You could attach hooks from the sides to hang bags of nuts or other feeders.

Position the table where you can see it, but also where the birds can see cats when they approach.

◀ You could add a bird bath, too. Just fill an old baking tin or tray with a little water, and put it on the bird table. The birds will always enjoy a good bath.

One point to remember is that you should not really feed the birds in spring and summer, as there will be plenty of their natural food available. This is better for the young and growing birds than bread and kitchen scraps.

Birdwatching

Birdwatching is an interesting and enjoyable activity in both city and country, and can become a life-long passion. Try it and see.

What you will need:

A pair of binoculars are useful – of the many sizes, the 8 × 30 mm ones are light and powerful enough for most purposes.

A notebook, pen and colored pencils – for notes and drawings of what you see.

A small tape-recorder – for recording either bird song or a commentary of what you see.

A reference book to identify what you see.

Some helpful hints

The best time to see bird activity is just before dawn, though dusk is a good time, too. Midday is when there is least activity.

Birds are more active in the breeding season (spring and early summer) than in the nesting season (mid-summer onwards). Some are more active again in autumn as they prepare to migrate.

When stalking: keep quiet, move carefully and slowly, use cover and camouflage, and concentrate on the birds.

When observing: find some cover, get comfortable, keep still and quiet, and be patient.

Much of this advice is useful when watching other wildlife, too.

Planting trees

On these pages you can learn how to choose, plant and maintain your own tree or trees. In doing so, you will improve the local environment and help wildlife by providing a vital habitat. Before you start, however, it is important you realize how much time and effort is involved. As well as the actual planting of the tree, there will also be several years of care before it can be left to itself.

What you will need:

A young tree (sapling) or trees

If you are growing trees from seed, you will also need: flower pots (or plastic containers with holes in the bottom), compost and a selection of tree seeds or seedlings.

A garden spade and fork

A strong wooden stake, about 5 ft long (only necessary if the sapling is over 3 ft high)

Wooden posts and protective wire fencing.

An adjustable rubber tie (from a gardening store)

Some mulch (wet straw, leaves, etc.) or peat

Planning your planting

To be successful, tree-planting must be carefully planned before anything is actually done. Several things need to be taken into account:

Where?
In your garden, your street, the school grounds, the local park or green, almost anywhere in fact. However, you will need permission from the relevant authority or landowner, unless it is your land. Make sure that nobody living nearby will object.

What sort of tree?
It is important to choose indigenous trees (those that are native to your area), as these will be better suited to the conditions and wildlife there. If you are planting near to buildings, roads or underground pipes, you should plant trees that don't grow too high. Their shorter roots are less likely to cause damage.

Will you need help?
Tree-planting is much easier if done by two or more people, though it can be done alone. If you are planting a lot of trees, or planting in public areas, it is best to get people from the local community involved. They can help by both planting the trees and looking after them afterwards. For advice, contact your local conservation group, council or gardening center.

Choosing your tree

The most satisfying way to raise saplings is to grow them from seed yourself, although this also takes the most time. Collect different types of freshly-fallen seeds in autumn and winter. Sow them in pots filled with moist compost, and wait for the spring. Some (like oak and beech) may germinate straight away, whilst others (like ash) won't germinate until a year later.

An acorn (seed) from an oak tree (native to Europe, Asia and North America) ▶

A beech nut and husk (native to Europe, though common in ◀ Asia and North America)

A capsule (containing seeds) from a eucalyptus tree (native to Australia) ▶

The other option is to buy the young trees ready-grown from a local nursery or garden center. This can be quite expensive, though it will give more immediate results.

These are points to look for when choosing a sapling:

Well-balanced branches

Strong straight stem

Plentiful, undamaged roots (these should be kept damp)

The smaller the sapling, the easier it will be to transport and the quicker it will grow.

Take care when transporting. Trees can die of "shock".

How to plant your tree

When growing from seed, you should plant the young tree outside once it has reached 5-6 ins (see picture). It will need a lot of protection for quite some time, so should be planted in a sheltered, protected spot.

Dig a hole the size of your pot, loosening the soil at the bottom (to help drainage). Remove the sapling and compost from the pot, put it in the hole, and keep it well watered.

It might be necessary to protect it with a fence (as shown).

When planting a larger sapling, you will ▶ need to prepare the hole more thoroughly (see picture). Though if it is under 3 ft high, you won't need the supporting stake.

Dig a hole the width of the roots and deep enough for the tree to sit in it up to its collar (where root and stem meet).

Break up the soil at the bottom of the hole with the fork.

Drive the stake (if needed) firmly into the ground, to about 15 in below the bottom of the hole.

Soak the roots well, ▶ and place the tree carefully in the hole. Shovel in some soil, shaking the sapling carefully to allow soil to get under and between the roots.

Firm gently with your foot. Add more soil and tread ▶ it down more heavily. Continue until the hole is filled and the soil is firmly trodden down.

The collar

Attach the tree to the stake with the rubber tie, and water the area well. Spread a layer of mulch or peat around the base of the tree (this prevents weeds from growing and also stops the soil drying up).

If there is any danger of damage (e.g. mowing-machines or grazing animals), put up a fence around the tree.

Looking after your tree

For the first few years, the tree will need some care and attention.

If you are planting on public land, get the local community interested, as they could help in maintaining and protecting the trees.

Make sure the tree is watered, especially in dry periods.

Keep the ground at its base as free of plants and grass as you can (they compete for water and minerals), but avoid chemical weedkillers.

Adjust the rubber tie and repair the stake and fencing when necessary.

It is important to remember, when choosing, planting and maintaining trees, that they should be treated carefully. Trees are complex living organisms and are easily damaged and killed. If well planted and maintained, they will give people pleasure, as well as providing food and shelter for wildlife.

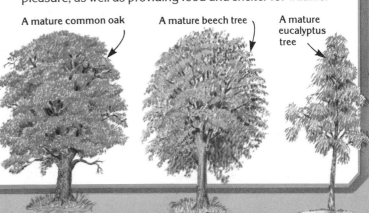

A mature common oak

A mature beech tree

A mature eucalyptus tree

Ecology projects

Making recycled paper

What you will need:

- Old newspaper
- Wire mesh (from a garden center or hardware store)
- Some absorbent cloths
- 2 buckets or bowls
- Wooden spoon or liquidizer
- Powder paint (to make colored paper)
- Plastic bag
- Weights, e.g. heavy books

What to do

Soak some old newspaper in a bucket overnight. The next day, drain off the extra water. Using the liquidizer (with permission if necessary) or your wooden spoon, mash up the paper and water into a pulp (and clean the liquidizer afterwards). Mix in the paint if you want colored paper.

Put the pulp into another bowl and add an equal volume of water. Mix these together. Slide the wire mesh into the mixture, lifting it out covered in pulp.

A windowsill salad garden

What you will need:

- Plastic margarine tubs
- Peat-based seed compost
- Some seeds (e.g. radish, parsley, spring onion, mint, etc.)

What to do

Fill the tubs with compost to within ½ in of the rim, and firm this down. Plant the seeds under ½ in of compost and water them. Place them on a windowsill in the kitchen, and water them once or twice a week. Herbs like mint or parsley can be used to flavor cooking (cut off small pieces with scissors when needed), and the radishes or spring onions can be pulled up and used in salads. You could then start growing other herbs (like basil, sage and thyme) or perhaps lettuce or a miniature tomato plant.

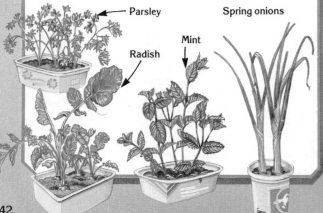

Parsley

Spring onions

Mint

Radish

Organizing your own group

If there is something you feel particularly strongly about (like cleaning up the litter in your area), you could try setting up a group to do something about it. The example here shows how you might create a pocket park on a piece of wasteland (see also page 25).

First, talk to your friends and see if they want to join in and help. Then try putting up notices or posters at school or in the library, telling people about what you want to do and how to contact you.

Prepare for your first meeting by noting down points for discussion, and ideas for action. It might be useful to invite an expert to give a talk or offer advice.

At the meeting, choose who is the chairperson (to make sure the meetings run smoothly), the secretary (to record decisions and inform members of future events) and the treasurer (to be in charge of money and accounts). You should also cover the first steps to take:

1 Find out who the land belongs to (ask your local authority), so you can get permission for your project.

2 Raise some money for things you may need to buy, e.g. seeds and shrubs. You could do odd jobs, or organize a raffle or sponsored walk.

3 Find out what help is available from the local authority or conservation group, and see what garden tools you can borrow.

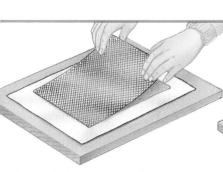

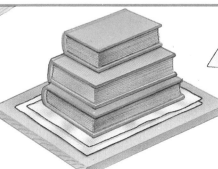

Lay a cloth on a clean, flat surface. Place the mesh (with the pulp side down) quickly and carefully onto the cloth. Press it down hard, then peel off, leaving the pulp on the cloth. Put another cloth on top and press down firmly.

Repeat these steps with your remaining pulp and cloths. When this is done, place the plastic bag on the top and weight the pile down.

After several hours (when the pulp has turned to paper), gently peel the paper off the cloths. Leave the pieces on some newspaper or kitchen towel until completely dry. The paper should now be ready for use.

Decide what each group member should do, and set a date for the next meeting.

Try to interest other people in what you are doing – get group members to write to the local papers, or put up notices or posters in libraries, schools and community or youth centers. Show how your work will improve the local environment and help its wildlife.

OUR CANAL IS A DISGRACE!
COME AND HELP US CLEAR IT.
CONTACT– J SMITH
TEL – 0375-919-7011

This is a poster about a canal clearing project. Try designing a poster about a pocket park.

You should have regular progress meetings until you are ready to start work on the site. Plan the layout, including perhaps a pond (see pages 36-37), some meadow (page 23) and plenty of trees (pages 40-41). Also, arrange to get rid of any large pieces of rubbish from the site (contact your local authority).

Working on your pocket park

1. Clear the ground of all rubbish, bricks and rubble.

2. If there is no topsoil, you can order it from a garden center. Mix it in with the soil already on the site.

3. After preparing the soil (digging it up, especially where it is compacted, and perhaps adding topsoil), plant plenty of seeds from different types of grass and wild flowers.

4. Make sure that you only use indigenous (native) plants, as these will support far more wildlife.

After everything is planted, you should keep working at the site – it will need to be maintained for quite some time (e.g. keeping it free of rubbish and protecting the young plants). All this hard work will certainly be worthwhile, once the park is set up.

If you want to get involved but don't fancy setting up your own group, you could join an environmental or conservation group. Many have their own local groups which organize activities, and they are always interested in new members (see addresses overleaf).

Going further

Below are some addresses of environmental, conservation and Third world development groups from around the world. Some are campaign groups (spreading information and influencing public, business and government actions), while others are involved in conservation work (like creating, maintaining and improving natural sites). Most have local groups which you can join.

International organizations

Friends of the Earth (FOE) – campaigns for protection of wildlife and habitats, and improvement of the environment at local, national and international levels. Youth section called Earth Action.

366 Smith Street, Collingwood VIC 3066, Australia

53 Queen Street, Room 16, Ottawa, ONT K1P 5CS, Canada

26-28 Underwood Street, London N1 7JQ, England

PO Box 39-065, Auckland West, New Zealand

530 7th Street SE, Washington DC 20003, USA

World-Wide Fund for Nature (WWF) (formerly World Wildlife Fund) – campaigns to protect wildlife and habitats throughout the world. Uses education to show the importance of the world's natural resources.

Level 17, St Martin's Tower, 31 Market Street, GPO Box 528, Sydney NSW 2001, Australia

35 Taraniki Street, PO Box 6237, Wellington, New Zealand

60 St Clair Avenue East, Suite 201, Toronto, ONT M4T 1N5, Canada

Panda House, Weyside Park, Godalming, Surrey GU7 1XR, England

1250 24th Street NW, Washington DC 20037, USA

Intermediate Technology – works on long-term development in poor countries, using technology appropriate to the needs of the rural poor. Aims to help people to become more self-reliant.

103-105 Southampton Row, London WC1B 4HH, England

777 United Nations Plaza, New York NY 10017, USA

Finding a local group

One way to find a local group is to check in your local telephone directory, under the heading "charities". Another method is to ask at your local library for information on local groups. But the best way to find out is to write to the organization's central office (some addresses are given below) and ask them whether there is an active group in your area.

Greenpeace – uses peaceful but direct action to defend the environment. Campaigns to: save the whales (see opposite), oppose nuclear power and weapons, stop acid rain and protect Antarctica.

134 Broadway, 4th Floor, Broadway, NSW 2007, Australia

Nagel House, 5th Floor, Courthouse Lane, Auckland, New Zealand

427 Bloor Street West, Toronto, ONT M5S 1X7, Canada

30-31 Islington Green, London N1 8XE, England

1611 Connecticut Avenue NW, Washington DC 20009, USA

Oxfam – involved in practical, long-term improvement of agriculture, health-care and social conditions in poor countries, as well as giving vital short-term emergency aid where and when it is needed most.

Community Aid Abroad, 156 George Street, Fitzroy, VIC 3065, Australia

251 Laurier Avenue West, Suite 301, Ottawa, ONT K1P 5J6, Canada

274 Banbury Road, Oxford OX2 7DZ, England

115 Broadway, Boston, MASS 02116, USA

Survival International – campaigns to protect surviving native peoples and the environments in which they live. Publicizes the risks to native peoples, and campaigns for their basic human rights around the world.

310 Edgware Road, London W2 1DY, England

2121 Decatur Place NW, Washington DC 20008, USA

National organizations

These organizations cover a variety of areas, including the environment, conservation and the Third World. Many will have local groups that you can join. If you are interested in further action, write to any of the addresses given here (including a stamp for return postage) and ask for information.

Australia

Australian Conservation Foundation, GPO Box 1875, Canberra, ACT 2601

Centre for Appropriate Technology, PO Box 795, Alice Springs, Northern Territory 5750

Rainforest Information Centre, PO Box 368, Lismore, NSW 2480

Total Environment Centre, 18 Argyle Street, Sydney, NSW 2000

The Wilderness Society, PO Box 188, Civic Square, Canberra, ACT 2608

New Zealand

Environmental Council, PO Box 10-382, Wellington

Nature Conservation Council, PO Box 12-200, Wellington

Royal Forest and Bird Protection Society, PO Box 631, Wellington

Tree Society, 41 Masterton Road, Rothesay Bay, Auckland 10

Canada

Canadian Nature Federation,
453 Sussex Drive, Ottawa, ONT K1N 6Z4

Ecology Action Centre,
1657 Barrington Street, Suite 520, Halifax,
Nova Scotia, B3J 2A1

Energy Probe / Probe International,
100 College Street, Toronto, ONT M5G IL5

Forests for Tomorrow,
355 Lesmill Road, Don Mills, ONT M3B 2W8

Sea Shepherd Conservation Society,
PO Box 48446, Vancouver BC V7X 1AZ

Society Promoting Environmental
Conservation,
2150 Maple Street, Vancouver BC V6J 3T3

Young Naturalist Foundation,
56 The Esplanade, Suite 306,
Toronto, ONT M5E 1A7

United Kingdom

British Trust for Conservation
Volunteers (BTCV),
36 St. Mary's Street, Wallingford,
Oxfordshire OX10 OEU

The Living Earth,
86 Colston Street,
Bristol BS1 5BB

Men of the Trees, Turns Hill Road,
Crawley Down, Crawley,
West Sussex RH10 4HL

The National Trust, PO Box 12,
Westbury, Wiltshire BA13 4NA

Royal Society for the Protection of
Birds (RSPB),
The Lodge, Sandy, Bedfordshire SG19 2DL

Scottish Conservation Projects,
70 Main Street, Doune, Perthshire FK16 6BW

WATCH, 22 The Green,
Nettleham, Lincoln LN2 2NR

United States

Defenders of Wildlife,
1244 19th Street NW,
Washington DC 20036

Food First,
1885 Mission Street,
San Francisco, CA 94103

National Audubon Society,
950 3rd Avenue,
New York NY 10022

Rainforest Action Network,
466 Green Street, Suite 300,
San Francisco CA 94133

Sierra Club,
330 Pennsylvania Avenue NW,
Washington DC 20005

The Wilderness Society,
1400 Eye Street NW,
Washington DC 20005

Greenpeace — saving the whales

One of the most famous campaigns by an environmental group was that of Greenpeace, when they attracted the attention of the world to the fate of whales in the 1970's. Some species, including the humpback, blue, fin and sperm whales, had been hunted to the edge of extinction, and whaling was still going on unchecked. Greenpeace activists confronted the whalers, preventing them from harpooning the whales. Their actions were captured on film, and shown to millions around the world on television news or in the papers.

The media coverage given to these actions resulted in growing public pressure to ban whaling. This, in turn, led to the 1982 decision of the International Whaling Commission (IWC) to ban commercial whaling for five years from 1985. However some countries have continued whaling since then, though on a smaller scale. Greenpeace are continuing their campaign against these whaling nations. They believe that after 50 million years of peaceful existence in the oceans, whales have earned the right to survive in peace.

By getting their inflatable craft between the whale and the harpoonist, the activists save the whale from a painful death.

Green politics

Many people believe that we must all make major changes in the way we live our lives if we are going to save the planet and ourselves from a harsh and difficult future. This view is put forward by "green" political parties all over the world, many of which are represented in their national parliaments. The West German green party (die Grünen), for example, increased their number of seats from 27 to 42 (out of 520) in the 1987 elections.

The green parties claim to offer an alternative to the usual political choices of the left, the centre or the right. They propose such things as a fairer sharing of the world's resources between rich and poor nations, and have far-sighted plans for the rebuilding of a new and better society. They believe that all governments should place people, the environment and the quality of life at the top of their list of priorities when making policy decisions.

Glossary

Acid rain. Rain and snow containing toxic chemicals which enter the atmosphere as industrial and vehicle **pollution**. It kills many living things, especially trees and freshwater plants and animals, and causes damage to buildings and people's health.

Adaptation. The process by which living things adjust to their environment, also any attributes they have developed to this end (e.g. a cactus spine is a leaf adaptation – with a small surface to conserve water).

Appropriate technology. Tools, machinery and methods that are suitable for use and maintenance by the people that use them (e.g. hand tools rather than tractors in areas where oil and spare parts cannot be obtained).

Biome. One of the large **ecosystems** into which the earth's land surface can be divided. Each is the **climax community** of a region with a particular **climate**.

Camouflage. The use of colour or patterns by a plant or animal to merge into its surroundings, or disguise itself as another plant or animal (**mimicry**).

CFC s (Chlorofluorocarbons). Chlorine-based compounds, used mainly in aerosols, refrigerator coolants and polystyrene, which are thought to be responsible for the slow destruction of the **ozone layer**.

Climate. Large-scale weather conditions (e.g. temperature, wind and humidity) that are characteristic of a certain region.

Climax community. A **community** that remains virtually unchanged, as long as there are no climatic or environmental changes (see also **Succession**).

Combined heat and power stations (CHP s). Particularly energy-efficient power stations, built in urban areas. They use the hot water produced by electricity generation to heat local houses, schools, etc.

Community. The plants and animals within a certain **habitat**.

Consumers. Organisms that feed on other organisms.

Crop rotation. A farming method in which different, specially-chosen crops are grown in one field each year over a four or five year cycle. It helps to control pests and avoid the depletion of minerals in the soil.

Decomposers. Organisms that live by breaking down dead bodies, releasing the minerals they contain.

Deforestation. Clearing trees for fuel or timber, or for farmland or new settlement land.

Desertification. The process by which **marginal land** (traditionally used for grazing by peasant peoples) is transformed into useless desert by overgrazing or other over-intensive farming methods, or by a **climate** change.

Ecosystem. A virtually self-contained system, consisting of a **community** of plants and animals in a given **habitat**, together with their environment.

Evolution. The long-term process of change in organisms, often occurring over millions of years.

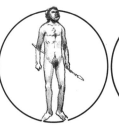

Extinction. The dying out of a species of living thing, and hence its complete disappearance from the earth.

Food chain. A chain of organisms, linked together because each is food for the next in line. Energy passes from one level (**trophic level**) to the next. All the food chains in an **ecosystem** are connected together in a complex **food web**.

Genetic engineering. Altering genes to create organisms that are useful to man. Genes carry information about an organism's basic characteristics.

Greenhouse effect. The trapping of the Sun's heat by atmospheric gases, causing the warming of the atmosphere. People's output of an increasing amount of these gases (mainly carbon dioxide) threatens to increase world temperatures more and more.

Habitat. A specific area, small or large, that is inhabited by a particular **community** of plants and animals.

Intensive farming. Farming by modern methods to maximize output, e.g. using artificial fertilizers, insecticides and other chemicals, and growing the same crop in the same field each year. These methods harm the soil and hence the natural cycles of the land.

Irrigation. The watering of land, mainly by using channels or ditches. Bad irrigation methods can make land infertile, e.g. by bringing up too much salt to the topsoil.

Marginal land. Land that is only just good enough for agriculture or grazing animals.

Natural selection. The theory of evolutionary processes first expounded by Charles Darwin. It suggests that those individual organisms within a species which have the best **adaptations** to their environment are the most likely to survive long enough to breed, hence these adaptations become established in later generations, and the species as a whole gradually "improves".

Niche. The position filled by a particular organism within its **ecosystem**, including its activities, such as feeding, and its relationships with other organisms.

Organic. Anything which is or was part of an organism (contains the element carbon).

Organic farming. Farming methods that work with nature's cycles, e.g. using **organic** animal waste (dung) as fertilizer, natural pest control, and **crop rotation**.

Ozone layer. A layer of the atmosphere containing ozone gas. This gas blocks out the sun's harmful ultra-violet rays, but man-made gases may be destroying it.

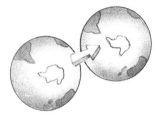

Photosynthesis. The means by which plants use the sun's energy to build their food (carbohydrates) from water and carbon dioxide.

Pollution. The contamination of an area, and its natural cycles, with unnatural substances or an excess of natural ones, and the consequent damage caused.

Producers. All green plants, which make food from simple materials by **photosynthesis**. They are the basis of all **food chains**.

Renewable energy. Energy from constant, natural sources, such as the sun, wind and waves.

Soil erosion. The process by which vital topsoil is lost (mainly blown away by wind or washed away by rain), having been loosened due to such things as **intensive farming**, **deforestation** and poor methods of **irrigation**. The land becomes barren.

Succession. The series of natural, progressive changes in an area, as one **community** replaces another, until a **climax community** is created.

Sustainable development. The use of methods of development that do not interfere with natural cycles or damage the ecological balance of an area (also sustainable forestry, farming, etc.)

Territory. An area occupied by one or more organisms and defended against incursion or attack by other other organisms (especially of the same species).

Trophic levels. Different layers of a **food chain**, each containing organisms which get their food and energy from similar sources.

Index

BOOK TWO

PLANET EARTH

Fiona Watt
Edited by Corinne Stockley
Designed by Stephen Wright

Illustrated by Kuo Kang Chen, Chris Shields and Aziz Khan
Scientific advisors: Steve Stone and Mike Collins

Contents

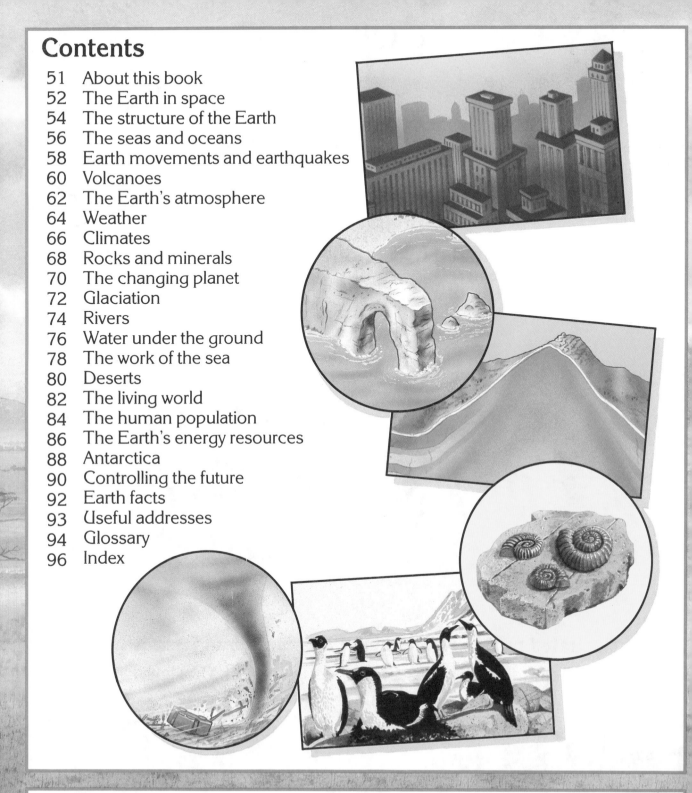

About this book

The Earth has gradually changed over millions of years to become the complex planet we know today. This book explains how many of the Earth's features and landscapes were formed, such as volcanoes, glaciers and deserts. It also looks at the various processes which continue to shape the Earth's surface, such as the action of rivers, the sea and the weather.

Throughout the book there are examples of many ways in which we use the Earth's resources, such as coal, minerals and energy from the Sun. It also shows the fragile balance which exists between the natural world and human activities. It looks at a wide variety of plant and animal species and how they survive in different environments around the world.

Using the glossary

The glossary on pages 94–95 is a useful reference point. It gives detailed explanations of the more complex terms used in this book, and introduces some new ones.

Useful addresses

On page 93, there is a list of addresses of museums and organizations who may be able to provide you with more information about the Earth and its resources.

Activities and projects

Special boxes like this one are found throughout the book. They are used for experiments and activities which will help you to understand different aspects of physical geography.

All the experiments and activities have clear instructions and are easy to do. You may need to buy some of the equipment at an electrical or hardware shop.

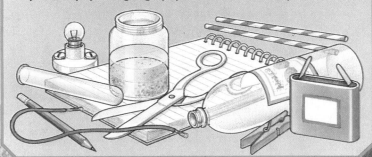

This scene shows an African grassland, or savannah, and some of the many species of animal which live there. Few people live in these areas because the climate is not suitable for farming. For more information about different climates, see page 67.

The Earth in space

The planet Earth seems enormous to us, but it is really just a tiny part of the Universe. The Universe consists of billions of stars, planets and moons, as well as vast areas of emptiness. No one knows how big it is, and astronomers think it is still expanding. They believe it was formed about 20,000 million years ago when all the matter, which was once packed together in one place, was thrown into space by a massive explosion. Galaxies formed in the clouds of dust and gas which spread out. It is thought that the Earth was formed about 4,600 million years ago.

Galaxies, stars and planets

A galaxy is an enormous cluster of thousands of millions of stars and planets. Galaxies can be different shapes, such as spirals. There are over 6,000 million known galaxies.

The Milky Way is a small part of one galaxy, but it is still made up of millions of stars and planets. It has a disc-like shape, formed by 'arms' spiralling out from a central cluster of stars.

The Solar System is a very tiny part of the Milky Way. It is made up of the Sun and the nine major planets. Each planet follows its own elliptical (oval-shaped) path, or orbit, around the Sun. Thousands of asteroids (balls of ice, dust and gas), also travel around the Sun.

The Earth is the fifth largest planet in the Solar System. From space it appears as a blue planet, covered with swirling clouds.

The Universe is so enormous that distances cannot be measured in the normal way, so they are measured in light years. One light year is the distance light travels in a year (9,500 billion miles).

The Sun is the center of the Solar System. It is not a planet, but a star. Stars send out light and heat energy. This is produced by chemical changes in the very center, or core, of the star.

The temperature and pressure in the core of the Sun are so high that hydrogen gas is turned into helium gas, giving off huge amounts of energy.

Mercury. Extremely hot, about 932°F in the daytime and −283°F at night. Almost no atmosphere. Rocky surface.

Earth. Temperature range of 140°F to −130°F. Atmosphere of mainly nitrogen and oxygen. 75% of surface covered by water.

Venus. Very hot, about 896°F. Thick, dense atmosphere — clouds of carbon dioxide which trap Sun's heat. Rocky, cratered surface.

Mars. Freezing temperatures. Atmosphere mainly carbon dioxide. Red, rocky surface.

Asteroids. Irregular-shaped lumps of rock which travel around the Sun.

The spinning planets

As each planet orbits the Sun, it rotates about its axis (an imaginary line running through it). The Earth spins around once every 23 hours and 56 minutes. Venus takes 243 Earth days to rotate, whereas Uranus takes only 11 hours.

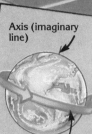

Axis (imaginary line)

The Earth rotates in this direction.

Exploring the planets

Exploration by unmanned space craft, such as the American space probes Viking and Voyager and the Russian probe Venera, has revealed information about the surface and atmosphere of the planets in the Solar System. From the information sent back from space, scientists have worked out what it may be like on each planet.

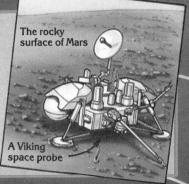

The rocky surface of Mars

A Viking space probe

Pluto. Smallest planet. Thought to have no atmosphere and thick icy crust surrounding core.

Neptune. Receives little light from Sun, so extremely low temperatures. Thought to have rocky core covered in ice crust.

Jupiter. Largest planet, mostly made up of clouds of gas and ice crystals. Atmosphere of hydrogen and helium. Tiny particles and rocks form a ring around it.

Uranus. Blue-green planet due to atmosphere of methane. Very low temperatures. May have solid core. Nine known rings circle the planet.

Saturn. Enormous ball of hydrogen and methane gas, with solid core. Circled by rings of thousands of blocks of ice.

The unique planet

The Earth is the only known planet where living things, as we know them, can exist. It is neither too hot nor too cold and contains just the right mixture of gases and water needed by plants and animals.

The Earth's atmosphere is the only one to contain nitrogen and oxygen. Living things need to breathe or absorb oxygen and nitrogen to build their cells. The atmosphere also helps to reflect harmful radiation from the Sun back into space.

Green plants use the Sun's energy to make their own food in a process called photosynthesis. Animals cannot make their food, so they must eat plants, or other animals.

Without the Sun's energy, life on Earth could not exist. The Earth is the only planet in the Solar System which receives the right amount of light and heat to support life.

A tropical rainforest supports thousands of species of plants and animals.

The structure of the Earth

The structure, atmosphere and natural life of the Earth have gradually changed, or evolved, since it was formed. The planet's rocks provide geologists (people who study rocks and their formation) with information about changes to the surface and structure of the Earth.

Inside the Earth

Inside the Earth are several layers of rock. One way scientists have worked out what these are like is by studying shock waves from earthquakes (see pages 58–59).

The crust is a relatively thin layer, between 3¾ and 43½ miles thick. It is thickest under mountains. The oceanic crust lies below the oceans and runs under the continental crust, which forms the land.

The inner core is solid and is made from iron and nickel. It is extremely hot (about 9032°F).

The outer core is made from molten (liquid) metal. As the Earth rotates, this layer moves around very slowly, producing the Earth's magnetic field.

The mantle is the layer of rock below the crust. It is about 1,863 miles thick. Areas of the mantle are so hot that the rock has melted to form a thick substance called magma (see page 60).

The Earth's crust

Ocean

Mountains

Oceanic crust

Continental crust

Mantle

Continental plates

The Earth's crust is divided into large pieces, or continental plates, which move around very slowly. If they move apart, magma comes up, cools and forms new rock. If they collide, they either rise up, or one is pushed below the other. Plates can also slide sideways against each other.

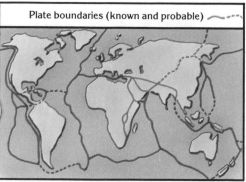

Plate boundaries (known and probable)

Plates moving apart   Plates moving together

Moving continents

If you look at a world map, you will see that the shapes of the continents seem to match each other like the pieces of a giant jigsaw puzzle. Some scientists think the continents were once joined together (about 200 million years ago), forming one massive land they call Pangea. They think the continental plates gradually drifted apart, making the land split up to form today's continents.

Evidence for the existence of Pangea comes from fossils, the remains of dead plants and animals preserved in rock. Fossils of the same creatures have been found on continents thousands of miles apart. For example, fossils of Lystrosaurus, a plant-eating reptile, have been found in South Africa, Asia and Antarctica. This suggests that these continents were once joined.

Some people do not think Pangea ever existed. They say that animals travelled across strips of land, or land bridges, which once existed between the continents. Others think they travelled across the oceans on clumps of floating plants.

Present positions of continents

Pangea

Movement of continents

Lystrosaurus

Hunting for fossils

Fossils are often found in rocks such as limestone, shale and slate. A good place to find them is where layers of rocks are exposed, for example where a new road is being built. Always ask permission before digging. You may also find fossils in the debris at the foot of a cliff. Differences in color, shape and type of rocks are all clues to look for. To get the fossils out, you will need a geologist's pick and a chisel. You could record your discoveries in a notebook.

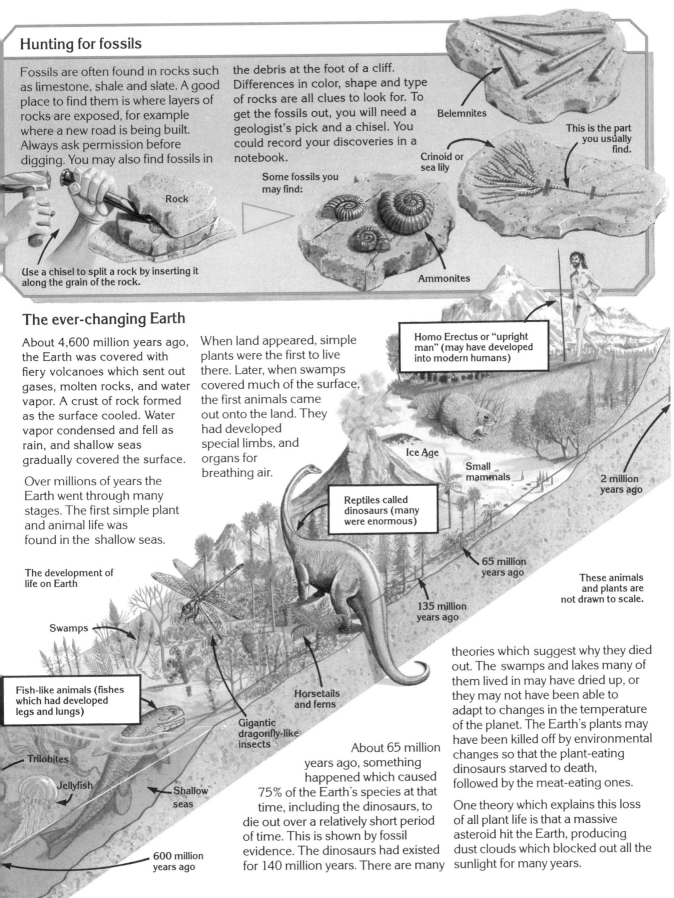

Rock

Use a chisel to split a rock by inserting it along the grain of the rock.

Some fossils you may find:

Belemnites

Crinoid or sea lily

This is the part you usually find.

Ammonites

The ever-changing Earth

About 4,600 million years ago, the Earth was covered with fiery volcanoes which sent out gases, molten rocks, and water vapor. A crust of rock formed as the surface cooled. Water vapor condensed and fell as rain, and shallow seas gradually covered the surface.

Over millions of years the Earth went through many stages. The first simple plant and animal life was found in the shallow seas.

When land appeared, simple plants were the first to live there. Later, when swamps covered much of the surface, the first animals came out onto the land. They had developed special limbs, and organs for breathing air.

Homo Erectus or "upright man" (may have developed into modern humans)

Ice Age

Small mammals

2 million years ago

Reptiles called dinosaurs (many were enormous)

65 million years ago

These animals and plants are not drawn to scale.

135 million years ago

The development of life on Earth

Swamps

Fish-like animals (fishes which had developed legs and lungs)

Horsetails and ferns

Gigantic dragonfly-like insects

Trilobites

Jellyfish

Shallow seas

600 million years ago

About 65 million years ago, something happened which caused 75% of the Earth's species at that time, including the dinosaurs, to die out over a relatively short period of time. This is shown by fossil evidence. The dinosaurs had existed for 140 million years. There are many theories which suggest why they died out. The swamps and lakes many of them lived in may have dried up, or they may not have been able to adapt to changes in the temperature of the planet. The Earth's plants may have been killed off by environmental changes so that the plant-eating dinosaurs starved to death, followed by the meat-eating ones.

One theory which explains this loss of all plant life is that a massive asteroid hit the Earth, producing dust clouds which blocked out all the sunlight for many years.

The seas and oceans

Almost three-quarters of the Earth's surface is covered by vast oceans and smaller seas. They supply the Earth's atmosphere with water vapor which rises to form clouds (see pages 64–65). They also influence the weather and climates of the world because winds are warmed or cooled as they pass over them.

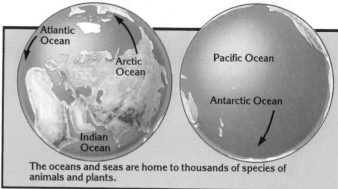

The oceans and seas are home to thousands of species of animals and plants.

The main ocean currents of the world

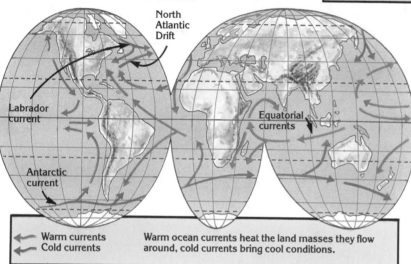

| Warm currents | Warm ocean currents heat the land masses they flow |
| Cold currents | around, cold currents bring cool conditions. |

Ocean currents

Ocean water travels around the world in currents. Surface currents form as the wind pushes the surface along. They follow the direction of the prevailing winds (the commonest winds which blow in an area). Warm currents flow near the surface where the Sun heats the water. Cold currents flow deep in the ocean, often moving in a different direction to surface currents.

All currents influence the climates of lands in their path. For example, Iceland lies in the flow of the North Atlantic Drift, or Gulf Stream, and is warmer in winter than places further south.

The ocean floor

The ocean floor has many mountains, hills, valleys and deep trenches. Many of the ridges and trenches run along the boundaries of the continental plates.

The longest mountain range in the world, the Mid-Atlantic Ridge, lies in the Atlantic Ocean. Along the ridge, molten rock rises through cracks in the ocean floor and solidifies or hardens, as it meets the cold water.

Deep trenches in the ocean floor occur where one plate disappears below another. The deepest trench, the Mariana Trench in the Pacific Ocean, plunges 36,188¼ feet below sea level. If Mount Everest (29,005 feet) stood in the trench, its summit would still not reach up to the ocean floor.

Tropical cyclones

Warm ocean currents can cause tropical cyclones (called hurricanes in America and typhoons in the Far East). These are fierce storms, with strong winds which form massive waves up to 82 ft. high. The moist warm air rises and cools, forming clouds.

Cooler air from the ocean surface rushes into the space left by the rising warm air and begins to spiral around. Wind speeds increase and land which lies in the cyclone's path is hit by the fierce storm.

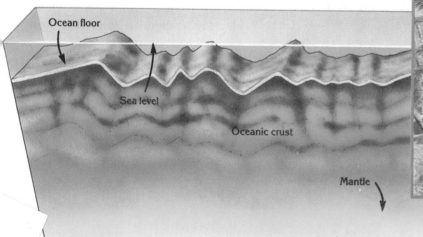

Ocean floor

Sea level

Oceanic crust

Mantle

Tropical cyclones can reach 198 mph

The frozen ocean

In the far north, ice covers much of the Arctic Ocean. When the water freezes, ice forms on the surface. As the wind blows, the ice moves and forms slabs, or floes. These join together to make a field of pack ice, hundreds of miles across.

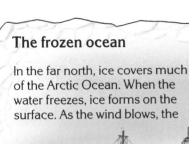

Ships which travel in polar regions have reinforced hulls to cut a path through the ice.

Volcanic islands

Underwater volcanoes are formed when molten rock rises to the surface through cracks in the oceanic crust and solidifies as it comes into contact with the cold, deep ocean water.

Where there are violent eruptions, large amounts of lava build up and the volcanoes appear above the surface as islands.

Surtsey lies on the Mid-Atlantic ridge.

Steam rising as molten rock meets the cold sea.

▲
Off the coast of Iceland, in 1963, fishermen thought they saw a boat on fire. It turned out to be eruptions from an underwater volcano. In just ten days, the volcano grew almost 656 ft. above sea level, forming a new island which was named Surtsey.

Volcanic island   Mountain range

Life in the oceans

Sea water contains oxygen, which is vital for all the animals which live in the oceans. The oxygen comes from seaweeds and phytoplankton (tiny single-celled plants). Like all green plants, these use the Sun's energy to make food, producing oxygen.

Because they need sunlight, all plants live near the surface of the oceans, so most animals live there too, as there is plenty of oxygen and food.

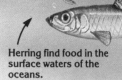

Herring find food in the surface waters of the oceans.

Seaweeds

No light from the surface reaches the depths of the oceans, so plants cannot live there. This means the deep water contains very little oxygen, so the animals which live there have special breathing systems. They feed on debris which falls from the water above.

Some fish have special light cells which they use to attract their prey or to find a mate. Angler fish have a light which dangles above their mouth.

No plants can exist at the bottom of the ocean.

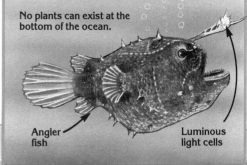

Angler fish   Luminous light cells

Trench

Earth movements and earthquakes

As the Earth's continental plates move together or apart, or slide sideways (see page 54), pressure, or stress, is exerted all across the layers of rocks which make up the plates. Although most rocks are hard, the pressure may cause them either to bend, making wave-like formations called folds, or to break, causing a line of weakness called a fault.

Folds

Folds occur when pressure which builds up in the crust makes the rock crumple up. This may happen at the plate edges or further inside the plates. The crumpled rock may rise to form mountain ranges, such as the Himalayas and the Alps.

Fold mountains

Earth's surface

Layers of rock

As pressure builds up, an area of crust is squeezed and the rock crumples and folds.

Faults

Faults are cracks, found throughout the crust. The major ones are found at plate boundaries. The main types are normal, reverse and tear faults.

Any movement of the plates has its greatest effect at faults because they are lines of weakness. If the pressure created by the movement is released suddenly, an earthquake may occur. San Francisco and Los Angeles both lie on the San Andreas fault, a tear fault in California.

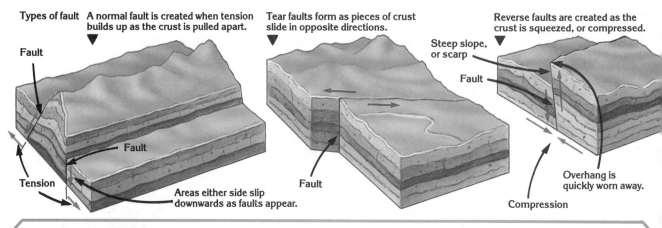

Types of fault A normal fault is created when tension builds up as the crust is pulled apart.

Fault

Fault

Tension

Areas either side slip downwards as faults appear.

Tear faults form as pieces of crust slide in opposite directions.

Fault

Reverse faults are created as the crust is squeezed, or compressed.

Steep slope, or scarp

Fault

Overhang is quickly worn away.

Compression

Making a vibration detector

Earthquake vibrations are detected by special machines. You can make your own vibration detector to use around your home.

What you will need

12 in. hacksaw blade
9 volt battery
Small light bulb and holder
3x4¾ in. lengths of single core wire (ask for help to strip ¾ in. at the ends)
Two pieces of wood (approx. 15¾ in. x 4 in. x ⅜ in. and 1½ in. x ¾ in. x ⅜ in.
A screw
A thumbtack
Strong glue

What to do

1. Stick the small block of wood to the larger piece, as shown.

½ in. Block 4 in.

¾ in.

15¾ in.

⅜ in.

Base

2. Wrap the stripped end of one wire around the screw, and screw one end of the hacksaw blade to the block.

Be careful with the sharp edge of the hacksaw blade.

Check that the blade vibrates.

Hacksaw blade

Screw

Wire

3. Wrap one end of another wire around the thumbtack and push it into the base below the free end of the blade. Attach the other end of the wire to the bulb holder.

Hacksaw blade

Light bulb

Thumb-tack Wire

Wire

Stick the bulb holder to the base.

4. Attach the last wire to the bulb holder (second connection) and the two loose ends to the battery. When vibrations make the blade touch the pin, the bulb will light.

Wire

You may need a weight (e.g. a coin) on the blade, to keep it close to the tack.

Wire

Battery

Earthquakes

Earthquakes occur when there is a sudden release of pressure, for instance when plates slip suddenly. The point in the crust or upper mantle where this happens is called the focus. Vibrations, or shock waves, pass outwards through the rocks.

Earthquakes have most effect at the epicenter, the point on the surface directly above the focus. They are often followed by weaker aftershocks as the rocks resettle. The areas most likely to suffer are those which lie on plate boundaries.

Every year over 500,000 earthquakes take place, but only a few cause severe damage. It is hard to predict where or when they will occur, although there are some signs which may come before an earthquake, such as a series of small shocks.

Measuring earthquakes

Seismologists (scientists who study Earth movements) use two different scales to measure earthquakes.

The Richter scale is based on the amount of energy produced at the focus. This is worked out using a seismometer, a device which measures surface vibrations. Each step up the Richter scale is about 30 times greater than the last.

The San Francisco earthquake of 1989 measured 7.1. It destroyed sections of the Bay Bridge and made the upper layer of an interstate road collapse.

The Mercalli scale is based on eyewitness observations (see below). The Armenian earthquake of 1988, which destroyed whole towns, rated 10.7 on the Mercalli scale.

The Mercalli scale

1 Not felt.

2 Felt by a few people, and on upper floors of buildings.

3 Hanging objects swing.

4 Windows and objects rattle.

5 Liquids spill, objects fall over.

6 Felt by everyone. Pictures fall off walls, windows break.

7 Difficult to stand, buildings damaged.

8 Towers and chimneys collapse.

9 General panic, cracks appear in the ground.

10 Severe damage to buildings and bridges.

11 Railway lines bend, underground pipes break.

12 Nearly everything damaged, large areas of land slip and move.

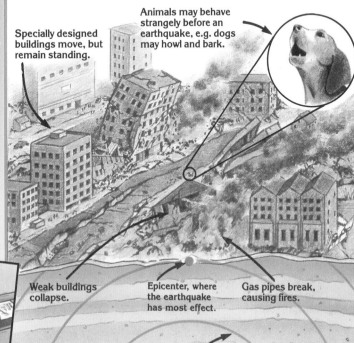

Animals may behave strangely before an earthquake, e.g. dogs may howl and bark.

Specially designed buildings move, but remain standing.

Weak buildings collapse.

Epicenter, where the earthquake has most effect.

Gas pipes break, causing fires.

Shock waves

As shock waves move away from the focus, they become weaker.

Focus

Tsunamis

When an earthquake's focus is under the sea, the vibrations create waves called tsunamis. These are often known as tidal waves, but they are not caused by tides. By the time they reach land they may be many feet high and cause severe flooding.

Tsunamis can cross oceans, causing damage to areas thousands of miles away from an epicenter.

Tsunamis up to 100 ft. high can crash onto coasts.

Volcanoes

Volcanoes, like earthquakes, are usually found in areas near the boundaries of continental plates. When pressure builds up below the crust, magma (molten rock) and gas are forced up into weak areas.

The magma may cool and solidify in the crust, or it may break through onto the surface, where it is called lava. It may emerge through thin cracks, called fissures, or be forced out through a wider pipe, where it builds up to form a volcano.

Inside an erupting volcano

Steam, dust and gas rise into the upper atmosphere.

Volcanic blocks and bombs (rock fragments thrown out from the volcano)

Falling ash

If the vent is blocked by solidified lava, a secondary cone may form on the side of the volcano.

Crater

Vent (above ground level)

When magma cools below the surface, dykes or sills may be formed.

Dykes are formed in near-vertical cracks which cut across layers of rock, or strata.

Sills are sheet-like formations which lie along the strata.

The shape of volcanoes

The shape of a volcano depends on the type of lava, how far it flows and the strength of the eruption. Viscous lava is thick and sticky, and cools quickly around the vent, solidifying and building up steep-sided cones. Non-viscous lava is thin, runny lava. It may flow for several miles before it cools.

When an eruption stops, magma in the vent and crater solidifies, forming a plug. Live volcanoes may be active, erupting fairly frequently, or dormant, resting for a long time between eruptions. Dead, or extinct, volcanoes will not erupt again.

Alternate layers of viscous lava and ash form steep-sided cones, called composite volcanoes.

Shield volcanoes are formed from non-viscous lava. They are low and flat.

The magma rises up the pipe and into the vent.

Pipe (below ground level)

Magma chamber

Types of eruptions

When pressure builds below the crust, gas and magma explode through the pipe and vent of a volcano. This throws out dust, ash and rocks. Sometimes an eruption will be so violent that the whole volcano blows up, leaving a large crater called a caldera.

Not all eruptions are violent. When the lava is runny, gases escape easily and the lava flows or spurts from the vent.

Shield volcanoes in Hawaii produce spurting fountains of runny lava.

The gases in viscous magma escape with force, causing an explosion in the chamber or pipe. Ash is thrown high into the air.

Predicting volcanic eruptions

It is difficult to predict when an eruption will occur, as each one is different. In the past, certain signs have been noted, such as bulges appearing on the side of a volcano, but nowadays more accurate predictions are possible. Scientists use satellites to detect "hotspots" below the surface.

Hot springs, geysers and fumaroles

In areas of volcanic activity, hot zones of the mantle lie relatively near the surface. Water in the ground is heated by the surrounding hot rocks. It bubbles up through cracks, forming hot springs.

Geysers are springs which send out jets of steam and water under pressure. Volcanic gases are given off from vents in the ground called fumaroles.

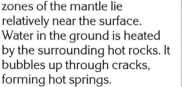
Geyser

Minerals which were dissolved in the water become deposited around the vent.

Fumarole

Hot springs

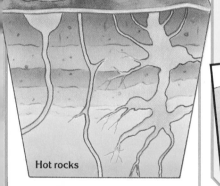
Hot rocks

Vesuvius

In AD79, Vesuvius, a volcano in Italy, suddenly erupted. Hot ash and poisonous gas spread over nearby towns and cities. One city, Pompeii, lay under 20 ft. of volcanic ash until it was discovered in 1711. The ash had protected the city, preserving the buildings and leaving things exactly as they had been when Vesuvius erupted. Vesuvius has erupted many times since then, but not as violently as in AD79.

People and animals died as they tried to escape from the ash and sulphur fumes.

Models were made by pouring plaster into the hollows left by the decomposed bodies.

Benefits from volcanoes

Rocks which come from volcanoes are known as igneous rocks (see page 68). Many contain valuable ores and minerals, such as diamonds, gold and copper. Despite the constant threat of eruptions, many people use the fertile soil on the slopes of volcanoes for farming.

Making a model volcano

To make a model volcano which will erupt safely, you will need baking soda (sodium bicarbonate), dishwashing liquid, three tablespoons of vinegar, red food coloring, a test tube or some other tube-like container, cotton balls and sand or fine soil.

What to do

1. Place a teaspoonful of baking soda in the tube. Add warm water so that it is a third full. Shake the mixture thoroughly.

Place your thumb over the end when you shake the mixture.

Test tube

2. Add five drops of dishwashing liquid and three drops of food coloring (to make your 'lava' look real). Mix the liquid.

Put some cotton balls in the neck of the tube.

3. Using the sand or soil, build a volcano round the tube, until it is level with the top.

The plug stops the sand getting into the mixture.

Sand or soil

Foam 'lava'

4. Remove the plug and pour in the vinegar from a small container. The new mixture will fizz up and out, like lava bubbling from a volcano.

The Earth's atmosphere

The atmosphere is a mixture of gases which surrounds the planet, stretching from the surface to over 560 miles into space. It protects the Earth from the harmful rays of the Sun and also contains the gases vital to all living things. The atmosphere traps heat from the Sun, warming up the air near the surface and creating the weather.

The composition of the atmosphere

The main gases which make up the Earth's atmosphere are nitrogen (78%) and oxygen (21%). There are also traces of carbon dioxide and other gases. Water exists in the atmosphere as water vapor, as droplets in clouds and as ice crystals.

The layers of the atmosphere

The atmosphere is divided into layers (though there are no sharp boundaries). The temperature changes through the layers (see below – read up from the bottom).

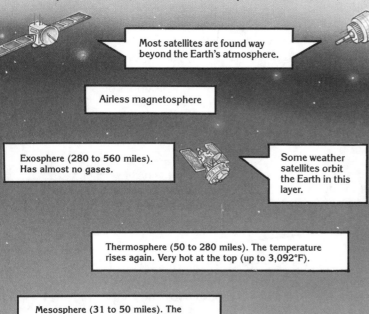

Most satellites are found way beyond the Earth's atmosphere.

Airless magnetosphere

Exosphere (280 to 560 miles). Has almost no gases.

Some weather satellites orbit the Earth in this layer.

Thermosphere (50 to 280 miles). The temperature rises again. Very hot at the top (up to 3,092°F).

Mesosphere (31 to 50 miles). The temperature falls with increasing height. Most meteors (pieces of rock from space) which enter the atmosphere are burned up in this layer.

Jet aircraft fly here, as visibility is good and there are few weather hazards.

Stratosphere (about 9 to 31 miles). It contains the ozone layer, a layer of ozone gas which absorbs the Sun's ultraviolet rays. This makes the temperature increase again.

Troposphere. Varies in height from the surface to between 5 and 9 miles. Weather forms in this layer, which contains most water vapor, wind and dust. The temperature decreases with height.

Air pressure

Although you cannot feel it, the layers of the atmosphere exert a force, or pressure, on the Earth's surface. Air pressure is greatest on the surface and decreases as you rise through the layers. It is affected by the temperature of the land or sea, so places at the same height do not always have the same pressure. Low pressure often brings wet weather, and high pressure is linked with fine weather.

Making a model barometer

Air pressure is measured on a barometer. To make a model barometer which shows changes in air pressure, you will need a wide-mouthed jar, a balloon, a drinking straw, a rubber band and some cardboard.

What to do

1. Cut the neck off the ▶ balloon and stretch the balloon over the mouth of the jar, so that it is taut.

Fix the balloon in place with the rubber band.

2. Cut one end of the straw to make a point. Fix the other end to the middle of the stretched balloon using some tape. ▶

Straw pointer

Make sure the straw is horizontal and that it is touching the balloon.

Tape

3. Place the cardboard behind the jar so that the pointer is touching the cardboard, and mark the position of the pointer. Draw a scale above and below this mark. Tape the cardboard to the jar, with the mark in line with the pointer. ▼

As the air pressure rises, the extra pushing force will push down on the balloon, and the pointer will move up the scale.

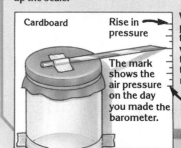

Cardboard

Rise in pressure

The mark shows the air pressure on the day you made the barometer.

When the air pressure falls, the air in the jar will push up on the balloon and the pointer will move down.

Fall in pressure

Movement of air in the atmosphere

Differences in temperature and pressure cause the air in the lower layers of the atmosphere to move, forming the world's winds. They blow from areas of high pressure towards low pressure areas. In many places there are local winds, caused by differences between the temperature of the land and sea. High mountains also affect local winds.

The main pressure belts and winds of the Earth

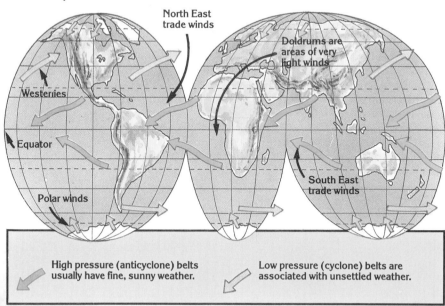

North East trade winds

Doldrums are areas of very light winds

Westerlies

Equator

South East trade winds

Polar winds

High pressure (anticyclone) belts usually have fine, sunny weather.

Low pressure (cyclone) belts are associated with unsettled weather.

The greenhouse effect

Heat energy from the Sun is trapped by carbon dioxide and other gases in the atmosphere. This process is called the greenhouse effect because it occurs in much the same way as glass traps heat in a greenhouse.

The amount of carbon dioxide in the atmosphere is increasing as fossil fuels (see pages 86–87) are burnt. World temperatures are rising as more heat is trapped. This is known as global warming.

Heat and light energy from the Sun enter the atmosphere.

The greenhouse gases trap some of the heat given back out by the Earth, increasing the temperature.

Ozone in the atmosphere

The ozone layer is found in the stratosphere. It is a layer of ozone gas which absorbs much of the Sun's ultraviolet radiation, preventing it from reaching the Earth.

Scientists have found that gases called CFCs (chlorofluorocarbons), destroy ozone gas. They are used in some aerosol cans and refrigerators. Holes have been discovered in the ozone layer above the Arctic and Antarctica. These may increase the amount of ultraviolet radiation which reaches the Earth.

Surface ozone is produced in the lower atmosphere, by a chemical reaction between sunlight and the exhaust fumes from cars. Normally it disperses through the atmosphere, but if a layer of cold air is trapped beneath warm air, it becomes concentrated and causes photochemical smog. Unfortunately, surface ozone cannot replace holes in the higher ozone layer.

Photographs taken from satellites show the hole in the ozone layer above Antarctica.

The size of the hole changes, but scientists think it is growing.

Efforts are being made to control the exhaust fumes from cars.

Air pollution has decreased since smokeless fuels were introduced in cities.

Photochemical smog causes eye irritations and some people find breathing difficult.

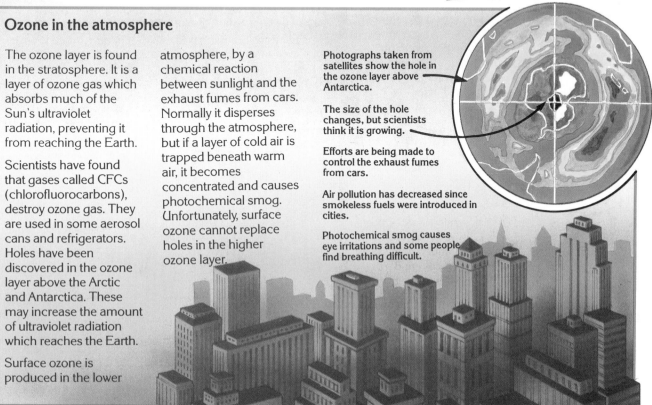

Weather

Weather is the daily condition of the atmosphere at a particular place at any one time. It changes from day to day and from place to place and is a combination of temperature, precipitation (rain, snow, sleet or hail), humidity (the amount of water vapor in the air), wind and sunshine. Winds are important as they help to circulate the air in the atmosphere around the world (see page 63).

The seasons

The seasons are caused by the amount of heat and light energy the Earth receives from the Sun. The seasons change due to the way parts of the Earth receive direct sunshine at different times of the year. The Earth is tilted at an angle, and as it orbits the Sun, a different half, or hemisphere, gradually receives more direct sunlight. It is summer in the hemisphere which receives most sunlight and winter in the other. Areas near the equator have no real variations in the seasons. This is because the Sun is almost directly overhead throughout the year.

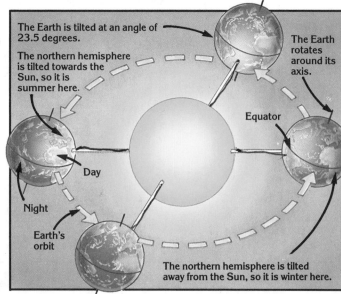

The Earth is tilted at an angle of 23.5 degrees.

The northern hemisphere is tilted towards the Sun, so it is summer here.

The Earth rotates around its axis.

Equator

Day

Night

Earth's orbit

The northern hemisphere is tilted away from the Sun, so it is winter here.

Making a rain detector

To make a detector that will buzz when it rains, you will need some tinfoil, a clothespin, a sugar lump, a buzzer, a 9 volt battery and 87 in. of single core wire cut into 2x3¼ ft. and 1x8 in. pieces (with ¾ in. stripped at each end).

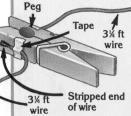

Peg

Tape   3¼ ft wire

3¼ ft wire   Stripped end of wire

1. Using tape, attach one 3¼ ft. wire to the gripping end of the peg, without covering the stripped wire. Attach the other 3¼ ft. wire on the other side.

2. Wrap a piece of foil around each gripping end of the peg to make two contact points. The foil must touch the bare wire.

Peg

Foil contacts

Peg

Foil contacts   3¼ ft wire

Terminals

3¼ ft wire   Buzzer

8 in wire

Battery

3. Attach one of the 3¼ ft. wires to the buzzer, and the other to the battery. Join one end of the 8 in. wire to the buzzer and the other to the battery. The buzzer should now go off.

4. Put a small piece of a sugar lump between the foil contacts. Put the peg outside and keep the rest of the detector inside. When it rains, the sugar will dissolve and the foil contacts will touch, setting off the buzzer.

The water cycle

When water is heated by the Sun, some of it evaporates. This means it changes into water vapor, which rises and mixes with other gases in the atmosphere. When moist air rises, it cools and the vapor condenses (changes back into a liquid), forming tiny droplets which join to make clouds. Depending on the air conditions, the water returns to the ground as rain, snow or hail. Snow forms at low temperatures, when tiny ice crystals join together.

Water falls to ground as rain, hail, sleet or snow.

Clouds rise and cool further. Water droplets get bigger.

Water soaks into soil and becomes ground water (see page 77), or runs across surface and into rivers, lakes and sea.

Water evaporates from surface of sea, rivers, lakes and land, and from plants.

Moist air rises and cools. Water vapor condenses to form clouds.

Clouds

Clouds are found at all levels in the troposphere (see page 62). Their shape, color and height give clues as to what kind of weather can be expected during the following hours or days. The main types of clouds are cirrus, cumulus and stratus. Not all clouds produce rain, or other forms of precipitation. If clouds move to a warmer area, the water vapor evaporates again.

Cirrus are high level clouds made from ice crystals.

Cumulus clouds may form puffy, fair weather clouds.

Stratus clouds form a thick, low level blanket of cloud, associated with light rain or drizzle.

Thunder and lightning

Thunderstorms occur when warm, moist air rises rapidly, forming tall clouds called cumulonimbus. Thunder and lightning are caused by a build-up of different electrical charges within these clouds. Once the charge at the base of the cloud gets to a certain strength, electricity is released as lightning.

Lightning heats the air it travels through and waves of air push outwards. They travel faster than the speed of sound, creating a sonic boom (like a supersonic aeroplane as it passes). This is thunder. Lightning tends to strike a high point, such as an isolated tree or a tall building.

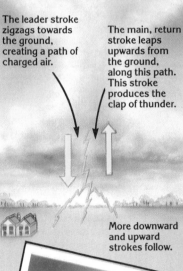

Cumulonimbus cloud

A flash of lightning is actually made up of a number of downward and upward strokes, all occurring within a fraction of a second.

The leader stroke zigzags towards the ground, creating a path of charged air.

The main, return stroke leaps upwards from the ground, along this path. This stroke produces the clap of thunder.

More downward and upward strokes follow.

Hail

Hailstones are small pellets of ice, formed when currents of air lift falling raindrops back to the top of a cloud. The raindrops freeze and receive several coatings of ice as they are carried up and down in the cloud by random air currents. They finally fall as hailstones.

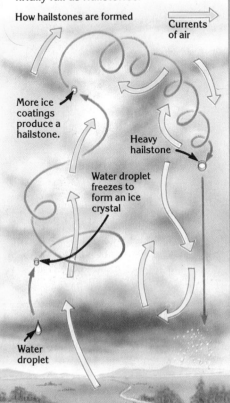

How hailstones are formed

Currents of air

More ice coatings produce a hailstone.

Heavy hailstone

Water droplet freezes to form an ice crystal

Water droplet

Weather hazards

Some types of weather may be very destructive. For instance, unusual amounts of rainfall may result in flooding or droughts. Severe droughts and famine have been experienced in Africa, when seasonal rainfall amounts were low and crops failed.

Floods caused by heavy rain often coincide with gales and high tides. Tropical cyclones (see page 56) cause severe damage, particularly at coasts.

Tornadoes are twisting whirlwinds, formed over land by hot air rising rapidly.

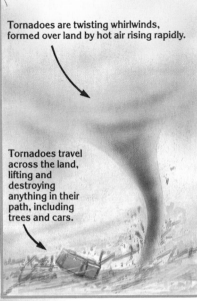

Tornadoes travel across the land, lifting and destroying anything in their path, including trees and cars.

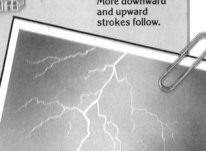

Climates

The climate of an area is the pattern of weather conditions experienced in that area over many years. One type of climate may affect a vast region or a small, local area, where it is called a microclimate.

Climates are affected by the distance from the sea, the altitude (height above sea level) and winds. The climate of an area determines the type of plants and animals found there. It also affects the lifestyle of the people.

Energy from the Sun

Most heat reaches the Earth's surface at the equator, where the Sun is directly overhead. The poles are much colder because the heat is spread over a greater area. The amount of energy any area of the Earth's surface receives from the Sun is called its insolation. Uneven heating of the surface causes movement of air and water vapor throughout the world, forming different climates.

North pole

Atmosphere

Equator

Rays of solar energy

Sun →

South pole

Solar energy travels a shorter distance through the atmosphere at the equator than at the poles.

The influence of oceans and seas

Ocean currents influence the climate of any land they pass (see page 56). During the day and at night, the land and sea gain and lose heat at different rates. This makes the air above them move, forming a coastal, or maritime, climate.

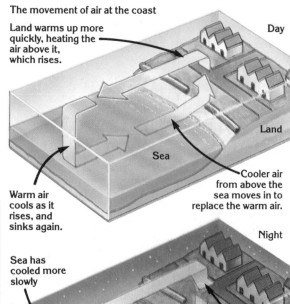

The movement of air at the coast

Land warms up more quickly, heating the air above it, which rises.

Day

Land

Sea

Cooler air from above the sea moves in to replace the warm air.

Warm air cools as it rises, and sinks again.

Night

Sea has cooled more slowly

Warm air rising

Cooler air moving out

Air cools and descends

Urban climates

Cities tend to be warmer than the area surrounding them. This is because concrete absorbs more heat than vegetation and retains it longer, making the nights warmer.

The ground beneath a city tends to be drier, as roads and pavements stop water draining into the soil.

Observing wind speeds

The wind affects the climate of an area. Its speed is measured on an instrument called an anemometer. To make a model anemometer you will need 3 plastic cups or yogurt containers of the same size, 3 knitting needles, a large cork, a long nail, 2 washers and a pole.

Knitting needle

What to do
1. Make two holes in each cup as shown, and push a knitting needle through.

Plastic cup

Holes

2. Push the points of the needles into the sides of the cork and push the nail down through the centre.

Nail

Cork

Knitting needle

3. Place the washers on the pole, and hammer the nail down through them.

4. On different days, record the number of times the cups spin round in a set time, e.g. 15 seconds. Find out the wind speed from a weather report and make your own wind speed scale.

Loosen the nail if the cork will not turn freely.

Hammer

Washers

Nail

Pole

You could paint one cup, to help you count the turns.

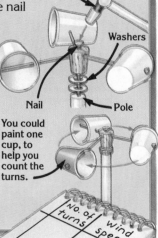

No. of turns

Wind speed

Mountain climates

On a mountain, temperatures decrease with altitude, giving different climates and vegetation at different heights. Trees cannot survive on high mountain slopes because there is little soil, which is often covered with snow, and there are frequent high winds. The direction a mountain side or valley faces (its aspect) also affects the climate. One side of a mountain may receive more sunlight than the other, which is nearly always in shadow.

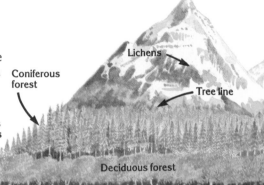

Lichens

Coniferous forest

Tree line

Different kinds of plants grow at different heights

Deciduous forest

Climates of the world

The different climates of the world determine the species of plants and animals found in different areas.

Climates also influence the way people live, their homes and their clothes. Where there are mountains in an area, the lower temperature high up will affect the climate and the types of living things found there.

Major climates of the world

Tundra

Winter temperatures low, averaging from –22°F to –4°F in coldest months. Low rainfall. Rise in temperatures in summer months, may even reach 63°F.

Snow in winter covers low-growing plants, such as lichens.

Polar

Extremely low temperatures with little rain or snowfall, making these icy areas frozen deserts. Animals depend on sea for food, so most wildlife found around coasts.

Animals are insulated by a layer of fat or thick fur.

Temperate

Seasonal variation in temperature, with rainfall throughout year. Temperature range generally between 21°F and 77°F. Coastal areas greatly influenced by sea. Winds cause day-to-day weather changes.

Deciduous trees lose their leaves in autumn when temperatures fall below 50°F, the minimum temperature needed for growing.

Deserts

Very low rainfall, less than 10 in. a year. Daytime temperatures in hot deserts may exceed 100°F. Not all deserts are hot — some are cooler in winter, or even frozen (see polar climate, above). Living things have adapted to life with little water.

Tuareg herdsmen of the Sahara wear loose clothes to protect them from the Sun and sandstorms.

Tropical grasslands

Warm throughout year. Dry and wet seasons alternate, often with droughts during dry season. Temperatures between 70°F and 86°F. Scattered trees, with grasses over 3¼ ft. high, which die in dry season.

Animals in the grasslands feed on trees as well as grasses.

Equatorial

Hot and wet all year round. High temperatures, never below 63°F. Climate provides ideal growing conditions for plants. Great variety of plant and animal species.

Cutting down and burning equatorial rain forests may be affecting world climates.

Rocks and minerals

The Earth's crust consists of layers of rock which have been formed over millions of years. The rocks on the surface are constantly shaped and worn away by water, ice and the wind, and by movements of the Earth's crust. There are three main types of rock, called igneous, sedimentary and metamorphic rock. Their formation and composition affect the relief, or landscape, of an area. They have an economic value as they contain fuels and precious minerals, and provide materials for building.

Minerals

All rocks are made of substances called minerals which vary in shape, size and colour. Most are made from a mixture of chemical elements, such as carbon, iron or silicon. Many rocks are made from several minerals, for example granite, which contains quartz, feldspar and mica.

Minerals may form regular, geometric shapes called crystals, for instance when molten rock solidifies or a liquid evaporates.

Diamonds are minerals of pure carbon, formed in an igneous rock called kimberlite in the upper mantle, under great heat and pressure.

Growing a crystal

Rocks are made up of many minerals and crystals of different shapes and colors. Below is an experiment with crystals which shows how they grow in size as liquid evaporates. Copper sulphate (from a chemist) is best to use.

Copper sulphate

Take care with copper sulphate, as it is mildly poisonous.

1. Pour 6¾ oz. of warm water into a jar. Add some copper sulphate and stir to dissolve it. Keep on adding until no more will dissolve (it sinks to the bottom).

Warm water

Jar

2. Pour the solution into a clean jar, leaving behind the undissolved crystals in a small amount of solution. Let this evaporate, then choose a large crystal and tie some thread around it.

Crystal

3. Tie the thread around a pencil. Place this across the top of the second jar so that the crystal is suspended in the solution.

Jar — Pencil — Thread — Copper sulphate solution

4. Leave in a warm place. Your crystal will grow as the solution evaporates.

Igneous rock

Igneous rock is formed when magma from the mantle rises, cools and solidifies. If it reaches the surface, the landform created, such as a volcano, is called an extrusive landform. If it cools inside the crust, the landform, such as a dyke or sill, is called an intrusive landform. In time, as the overlying rock is worn away, intrusive landforms may appear on the surface.

Igneous rock contains closely-packed crystals, formed as the magma cools. Large crystals are found in rocks such as granite, which forms when magma cools slowly below the surface. If it cools quickly, minute crystals are formed, making rock such as obsidian.

When a vast amount of magma rises and cools within the Earth's crust, it may form a massive intrusive landform called a batholith.

Batholiths, often made of granite, may be exposed after the Earth's surface has been eroded away.

A tor is part of a batholith which has been exposed.

Batholiths may be hundreds of miles in area.

Sedimentary rock

Sediments are materials which have collected together as a result of natural processes. For example, when a rock is worn away by water, wind or ice, the particles may be carried away and deposited elsewhere, forming a sediment.

Sedimentary rock is formed from sediments. Layers of sediment gradually build up until the bottom layers are squeezed and cemented together, forming a layer of rock called a stratum. This process often continues, producing many layers of rock.

The weight of the top layers exerts pressure on the layers below.

Layers of sediment

The pressure squeezes the particles and they are cemented together, forming new rock.

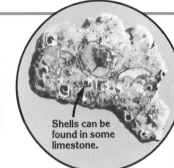

Shells can be found in some limestone.

The type of rock formed depends on the nature of the sediment. Instead of eroded rock particles (which form rock such as sandstone), the sediment could be deposits left behind when water evaporated (which form rock salt). It could also be the remains of plants or animals (which form coal and limestone).

Metamorphic rock

Metamorphic rock is formed when igneous or sedimentary rock is altered by heat or pressure, or both. It can be formed in a small area, when magma comes into contact with other rocks, or on a large scale, such as during mountain building. Some examples are slate, formed from mud and a rock called shale, and marble, formed from limestone.

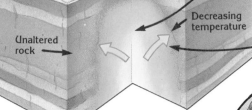

Extremely hot magma is forced into the surrounding rock (e.g. sedimentary rock).

The texture, color and chemical composition of the minerals in the rock are altered by the heat.

Decreasing temperature

Unaltered rock

Slightly altered rock (metamorphic rock)

During the formation of mountains (see page 48), rocks are under great pressure.

The temperature of the rock may also rise due to the friction caused by movement.

Schist is a metamorphic rock formed during mountain building.

The pressure and temperature changes cause metamorphic rock to be formed over a vast area.

The composition of rocks

The arrangement and type of minerals found in different rocks give them certain qualities, which affect the way they are worn away.

Pervious rocks, such as limestone, for example, have cracks which let water through. Porous rocks, such as sandstone, have spaces between each tiny particle, and water passes through these. These are both types of permeable rock (see page 76). Impermeable rocks do not let water pass through easily.

In the Grand Canyon, layers of sedimentary rock, such as sandstone, have been revealed as the Earth's surface has been worn away.

The layers of rock have been shaped by the action of water.

The changing planet

When rock is exposed to the atmosphere, its surface is gradually broken down by various processes called weathering. There are two main types of weathering, called mechanical and chemical weathering, and most rocks are broken down by a combination of these processes. Rock material which has been weakened and broken off by weathering is called debris. It is carried away and broken down further by various forces. During this process, called erosion, the debris grinds against other rocks, breaking off more debris. Further erosion of debris may turn it into soil.

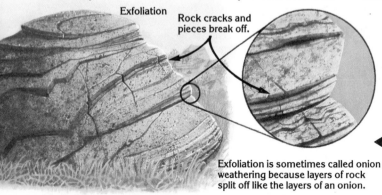

Exfoliation

Rock cracks and pieces break off.

Exfoliation is sometimes called onion weathering because layers of rock split off like the layers of an onion.

Mechanical weathering

In the day, the Sun heats rock surfaces and the minerals expand. At night, temperatures fall and the minerals contract. Most rocks contain several minerals, which expand and contract at different rates, making the surface crumble and break up. This is the main type of mechanical weathering.

◀ If rocks contain only one mineral, whole areas of the surface expand and contract together and eventually peel off. This is called exfoliation.

In cold areas, rocks which contain ▶ cracks, or fractures, may also be broken by a process known as freeze-thaw. If water enters the cracks and freezes, it expands as it turns to ice.

The ice exerts great pressure within the rock and forces the cracks apart. If the temperature rises, the ice melts, only to freeze again if it falls. In time, pieces of rock break off.

Water enters cracks and freezes, gradually forcing them apart.

Freeze-thaw action breaks off pieces of rock.

Debris accumulates and may form a scree slope. This may slide due to gravity.

Scree slope

The effect of freezing

By freezing some clay, you can demonstrate the effects of freeze-thaw action. You will need two lumps of moist clay (one to act as a comparison), some plastic food wrap and the use of a freezer. You can buy clay from a craft shop but try using some soil from your garden as it may contain clay.

What to do

1. Squeeze both lumps of clay to get rid of any air bubbles and make them compact.

2. Wrap the lumps individually in plastic food wrap. Place one lump of clay in the freezer and the other one on a window sill. Leave them there overnight.

Window sill

Freezer

Plastic food wrap

3. Take the clay out of the freezer and remove the plastic wrap. As the clay thaws, compare it with the lump from the window sill. The cracks in the thawed clay are due to freeze-thaw action.

Clay left on the window sill

Clay from the freezer

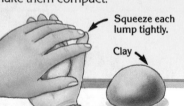

Squeeze each lump tightly.

Clay

Chemical weathering

Chemical weathering occurs when minerals are eaten away by chemicals, such as those in rain. As it forms, rain absorbs gases from the air, making a weak acid which attacks the rock.

In rocks such as limestone, rainwater gets into cracks, making them bigger (see page 77).

Chemicals in rainwater attack and gradually eat away the rock.

Acid rain

Acid rain is caused by air
pollution. The burning of
fossil fuels such as coal
and oil gives off gases
containing sulphur and
nitrogen. These react
with water droplets in the
air, making the rainwater
more acidic.

Acid rain breaks down the
waxy coating on plant
leaves and also enters the
plants through their roots.

Acid rain falls on the soil
and enters rivers and lakes,
killing wildlife.

Acid rain makes chemical
weathering worse. In cities,
it is causing serious
damage
to old
buildings
and
statues.

Power stations release large
amounts of gases into the
atmosphere.

Clouds containing acid droplets
may travel great distances.

Weathering by plants and animals

Plants and animals help to break
down rocks by both mechanical
and chemical weathering.

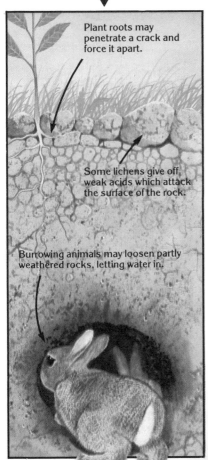

Plant roots may
penetrate a crack and
force it apart.

Some lichens give off
weak acids which attack
the surface of the rock.

Burrowing animals may loosen partly
weathered rocks, letting water in.

Erosion

Erosion occurs after fragments of
rock, or debris, have been produced
by weathering. Agents of erosion,
such as water, ice and the wind, pick
up and carry away the debris. As it is
carried, it is constantly grinding
against other rocks, wearing away
these rocks and being worn into finer
particles itself. Finally, it is deposited in
a new place.

Rivers
Rivers carry a
great deal of
debris, which
erodes the bed
and the banks.
When the river
becomes too
slow to carry the
debris, it is
deposited.

The sea
Waves pick up
pebbles and
sand and smash
them against
cliffs, eroding the
cliffs. They also
move sand and
debris along the
shore (see pages
78–79).

Ice
In cold areas,
debris is frozen
into glaciers. As
the ice moves
downhill, the
debris scrapes
against rocks,
eroding their
surface (see
pages 72–73).

The wind
The wind picks
up fine particles
and blasts them
against rocks,
eroding the
rocks. It has a
particularly
powerful effect in
desert areas.

Speeding up erosion

Erosion has been accelerated by
man's activities. For instance, soil
erosion by wind and water is a
problem in many areas.

Large areas of vegetation are cleared for farming or
other reasons.

The roots of the plants no longer bind together the
top layers of soil (see also page 75).

The wind blows away the
topsoil, leaving barren areas
called dust bowls.

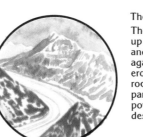

Glaciation

During the last million years, the Earth's climate has changed several times. At certain times, it became much colder, resulting in ice ages. Areas of the surface were covered in ice, until temperatures rose again and most of the ice melted. The last main ice age was about 20,000 years ago, but some areas of the Earth's surface are still covered by thick, moving layers of ice, called glaciers.

Where glaciers are found

The largest glaciers are ice sheets, found in Greenland and Antarctica and in areas which have very cold winters and cool summers. Other glaciers, called valley glaciers, can be found in high mountain regions, such as the Alps and the Rockies, where there is snow all year.

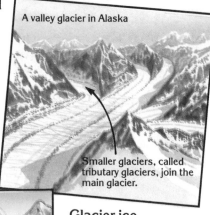
A valley glacier in Alaska

Smaller glaciers, called tributary glaciers, join the main glacier.

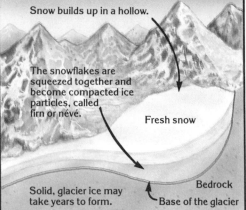
Snow builds up in a hollow.

The snowflakes are squeezed together and become compacted ice particles, called firn or névé.

Fresh snow

Solid, glacier ice may take years to form.

Bedrock

Base of the glacier

Glacier ice

Glaciers are formed when snow does not melt in the summer and builds up in hollows. The pressure of the layers of snow crushes the snow crystals and turns them into compacted ice particles, like snow which has been squeezed to make a snowball.

The moving glacier

Glaciers move because they are on sloping ground. The weight of the ice makes them move downhill, pressing on the rock beneath (bedrock). Their speed depends on the steepness of the slope, the amount of snow which falls and the thickness of the ice. Some valley glaciers flow as much as 328 ft. in a year, but in areas which are almost flat and have little snowfall, the glaciers (ice sheet glaciers) may move less than one inch.

In Greenland and Antarctica, ice sheets flow slowly down into the sea, where enormous blocks break off, forming icebergs.

Making a model glacier

As a glacier moves, friction is created as the debris grinds against the bedrock. This makes the ice move more slowly than it would do without debris. You can show this in a simple experiment, using two plastic containers (e.g. margarine tubs), some gravel or some rough stones, a piece of wood (approx. 17¾ in. x 6 in.), a cardboard box, a freezer and some water.

What to do

1. Half-fill your containers with cold water. Add gravel or small stones to one of them, so that the bottom is covered. Top up the other container so they are filled to the same level.

Containers

Gravel

Freezer

2. Place both containers in a freezer, making sure they are level. Leave them to freeze solid.

3. Remove the containers from the freezer and turn out your two glacier blocks. Before testing them, let them stand for ten minutes.

Glacier blocks

Ice

Gravel

4. Lean the piece of wood against the box to act as your mountain slope and test both your glaciers to see which one moves more easily. You should find that your glacier with gravel moves more slowly because of friction.

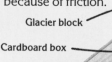
Glacier block

Cardboard box

Wood

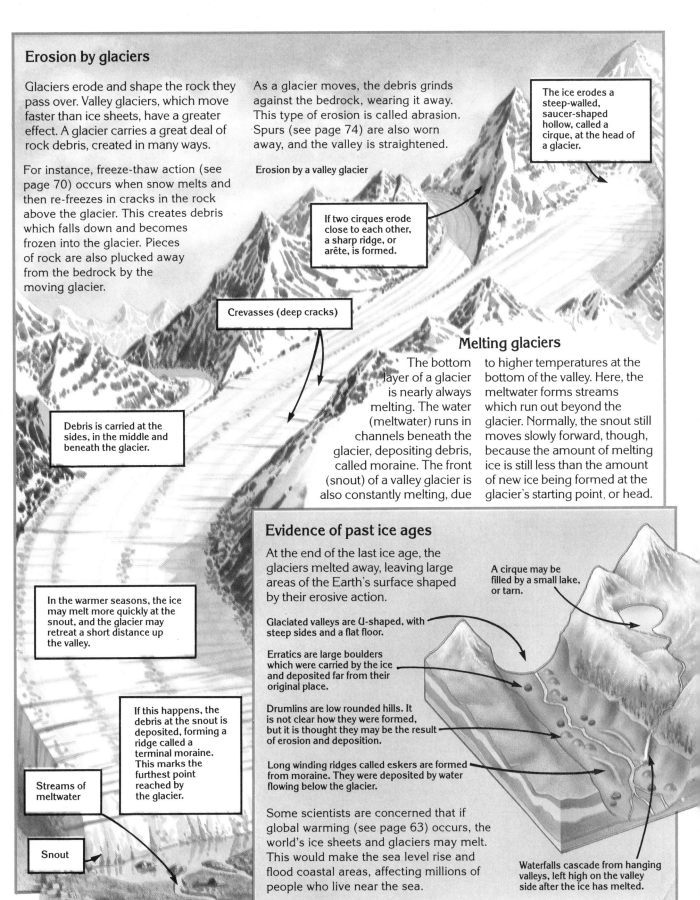

Erosion by glaciers

Glaciers erode and shape the rock they pass over. Valley glaciers, which move faster than ice sheets, have a greater effect. A glacier carries a great deal of rock debris, created in many ways.

For instance, freeze-thaw action (see page 70) occurs when snow melts and then re-freezes in cracks in the rock above the glacier. This creates debris which falls down and becomes frozen into the glacier. Pieces of rock are also plucked away from the bedrock by the moving glacier.

As a glacier moves, the debris grinds against the bedrock, wearing it away. This type of erosion is called abrasion. Spurs (see page 74) are also worn away, and the valley is straightened.

Erosion by a valley glacier

The ice erodes a steep-walled, saucer-shaped hollow, called a cirque, at the head of a glacier.

If two cirques erode close to each other, a sharp ridge, or arête, is formed.

Crevasses (deep cracks)

Debris is carried at the sides, in the middle and beneath the glacier.

Melting glaciers

The bottom layer of a glacier is nearly always melting. The water (meltwater) runs in channels beneath the glacier, depositing debris, called moraine. The front (snout) of a valley glacier is also constantly melting, due to higher temperatures at the bottom of the valley. Here, the meltwater forms streams which run out beyond the glacier. Normally, the snout still moves slowly forward, though, because the amount of melting ice is still less than the amount of new ice being formed at the glacier's starting point, or head.

In the warmer seasons, the ice may melt more quickly at the snout, and the glacier may retreat a short distance up the valley.

If this happens, the debris at the snout is deposited, forming a ridge called a terminal moraine. This marks the furthest point reached by the glacier.

Streams of meltwater

Snout

Evidence of past ice ages

At the end of the last ice age, the glaciers melted away, leaving large areas of the Earth's surface shaped by their erosive action.

Glaciated valleys are U-shaped, with steep sides and a flat floor.

Erratics are large boulders which were carried by the ice and deposited far from their original place.

Drumlins are low rounded hills. It is not clear how they were formed, but it is thought they may be the result of erosion and deposition.

Long winding ridges called eskers are formed from moraine. They were deposited by water flowing below the glacier.

Some scientists are concerned that if global warming (see page 63) occurs, the world's ice sheets and glaciers may melt. This would make the sea level rise and flood coastal areas, affecting millions of people who live near the sea.

A cirque may be filled by a small lake, or tarn.

Waterfalls cascade from hanging valleys, left high on the valley side after the ice has melted.

Rivers

Streams and rivers shape the Earth's surface by wearing away the rock they flow over and by depositing large amounts of material. The shape of a river valley changes along the upper, middle and lower stages of its course. Throughout the world, rivers are important for supplying water, transporting goods and producing energy.

Transportation and deposition

All the material (sediment) transported by a river is called its load. The heaviest rocks and pebbles are rolled and bounced along the river bed, becoming round and smooth due to contact with each other and the river bed. This process is called attrition. Finer particles of clay and silt are carried along above the heavier ones. They are suspended in the water. Some minerals travel in solution, that is, they are dissolved.

A river deposits its load as it slows down. The largest material is deposited first, followed by the smaller particles. The fine sediment may be carried as far as the river mouth.

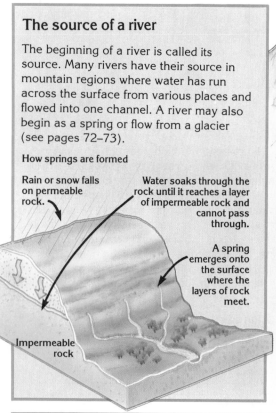

The source of a river

The beginning of a river is called its source. Many rivers have their source in mountain regions where water has run across the surface from various places and flowed into one channel. A river may also begin as a spring or flow from a glacier (see pages 72–73).

How springs are formed

Rain or snow falls on permeable rock.

Water soaks through the rock until it reaches a layer of impermeable rock and cannot pass through.

A spring emerges onto the surface where the layers of rock meet.

Impermeable rock

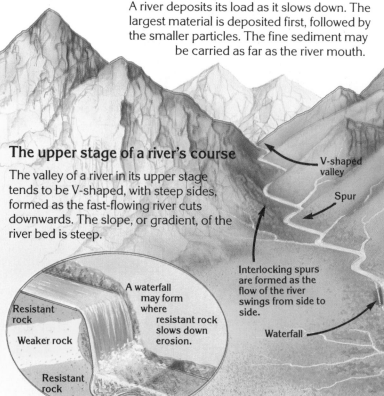

The upper stage of a river's course

The valley of a river in its upper stage tends to be V-shaped, with steep sides, formed as the fast-flowing river cuts downwards. The slope, or gradient, of the river bed is steep.

V-shaped valley

Spur

Interlocking spurs are formed as the flow of the river swings from side to side.

Waterfall

A waterfall may form where resistant rock slows down erosion.

Resistant rock

Weaker rock

Resistant rock

Erosion by rivers

Running water erodes rock by the constant movement of the pebbles and particles of sand it carries. The amount of erosion depends on the volume and speed of the water, and the composition of the rock.

Most erosion happens early in a river's course, as the fast-flowing water carries large amounts of material. Some rock, such as sandstone, is eroded more quickly than resistant rock, such as granite.

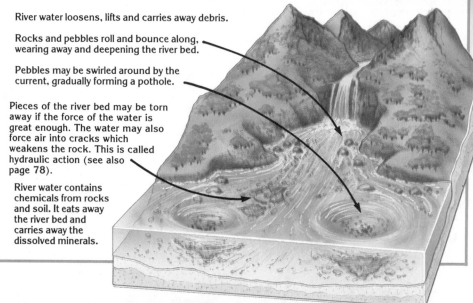

River water loosens, lifts and carries away debris.

Rocks and pebbles roll and bounce along, wearing away and deepening the river bed.

Pebbles may be swirled around by the current, gradually forming a pothole.

Pieces of the river bed may be torn away if the force of the water is great enough. The water may also force air into cracks which weakens the rock. This is called hydraulic action (see also page 78).

River water contains chemicals from rocks and soil. It eats away the river bed and carries away the dissolved minerals.

Pollution in rivers

Many rivers around the world suffer from pollution. In many areas, chemical waste from factories, and sometimes untreated sewage, is pumped into them. Rainwater falling on fields often becomes contaminated by chemicals such as pesticides. It drains into streams and rivers, killing animal and plant life.

Birds are poisoned when they eat contaminated fish or plants from a polluted river.

The middle stage

In the middle stage, the river's slope, or gradient, becomes more gentle and its speed begins to decrease. The valley becomes wider as the river erodes sideways.

The river begins to meander, or flow from side to side in long, looping bends.

The bends are also called meanders.

The lower stage

The volume of water increases in the river's lower stage, as other rivers, called tributaries, join it. It slows down, as the gradient is more gentle, and meanders across the valley floor, depositing sediments. Finally, it flows into the sea or a lake.

If the river floods, the water flows out sideways onto the plain and deposits its load, which is then called alluvium. The largest sediments are deposited first, forming banks or levees, which are seen when the water recedes.

The fine sediments are deposited over a larger area, leaving fertile soil after the water drains off.

Flat valley floor (flood plain)

Delta

Looking at sediments

A river deposits sediment by weight — the heaviest first, followed by lighter and lighter material. You can show this, using a plastic bottle, about 2 ft. of plastic tubing, some soil, water, tape and a plastic funnel (or one made from cardboard).

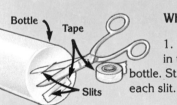

Bottle

Tape

Slits

What to do

1. Cut two ¾ in. slits in the bottom of the bottle. Stick some tape over each slit.

2. Use your funnel to half-fill the bottle with soil. Then almost fill the bottle with water. Screw on the lid, shake vigorously, and leave to stand for 24 hours.

Card funnel

3. Unscrew the lid and place one end of the tubing into the water. Suck the water up, put your thumb over the end and bend the tube downwards, into a container. Remove your thumb and the water will drain out.

Soil

Plastic tubing

Container

Water

Make sure you don't swallow any water.

4. Pull the tape off the slits and leave for another 24 hours. This allows any remaining water to drain away. You should now see the layers of sediment. To look closely, carefully cut the bottle in half.

Bottle cut away

Layers of sediment

If the soil is very sandy, the sample will crumble. A clay soil will hold together well.

Deltas

As a river flows into the sea, it slows down further, and any sediment it is still carrying is deposited. If the sediment is deposited faster than it is washed away by the currents and tide, it builds up an area of flat land at the mouth of the river, called a delta. The river splits up into narrower channels as it crosses the delta and finds its way to the sea. This creates a number of islands of sediment in the delta. Many people live and farm on the fertile ▶ sediments which make up delta islands. In Bangladesh, millions of people live on islands formed in the delta of the River Ganges. They grow rice and keep cattle, despite a constant risk from flooding.

On several occasions, tropical cyclones in the Ganges delta have caused severe flooding, killing millions of people.

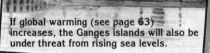

If global warming (see page 63) increases, the Ganges islands will also be under threat from rising sea levels.

Water under the ground

Rain falling on the Earth's surface may run into a river, evaporate back into the atmosphere, or soak into the soil. If the water soaks into the soil it may be absorbed into the layers of rock underneath, depending on their composition.

Water in rocks

Water travels slowly through porous rock which has tiny spaces between its grains, or through pervious rock which has joints or small cracks in it. Any rock which allows water to pass through it is said to be permeable. Water enters permeable rock and moves downward due to gravity until it reaches a layer of impermeable rock (see page 69).

Porous rock, e.g. chalk
Tiny grains of rock
Water travels slowly through the spaces between the grains.

Pervious rock, e.g. limestone
Chunks of rock
Vertical crack (joint)
Horizontal crack (bedding plane)
Water travels along the cracks

Water storage underground

Water which seeps down through soil and enters rock is known as ground water. It stops when it reaches an impermeable layer, and the permeable rock becomes saturated (full of water). The highest level of the water in saturated rock is called the water table.

Any layer of permeable rock is called an aquifer. In some parts of the world, aquifers cover thousands of kilometres.

Aquifer
Saturated rock
Water seeps down
Water table
Impermeable rock
Rivers may be found where an aquifer is at the surface.

Bringing ground water to the surface

If a well is dug below the level of the water table, ground water soaks into it. If the level of the water table falls, the well dries up.

Normally, water has to be pulled or pumped up from a well, but if there is enough water pressure in the aquifer, water will be pushed out of the well. This kind of well is called an artesian well.

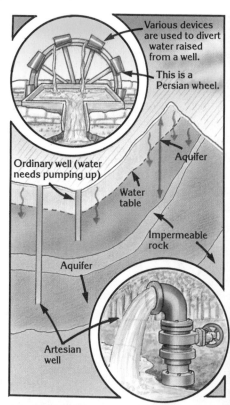

Various devices are used to divert water raised from a well.
This is a Persian wheel.
Ordinary well (water needs pumping up)
Aquifer
Water table
Impermeable rock
Aquifer
Artesian well

Water in a desert

Rain in a desert is very scarce (see page 80), but moist areas, called oases, can be found where groundwater reaches the surface. The water travels underground to the oasis, in an aquifer which is supplied with rain a long way away. Some oases may be over a thousand miles from the area where the rainwater entered the aquifer.

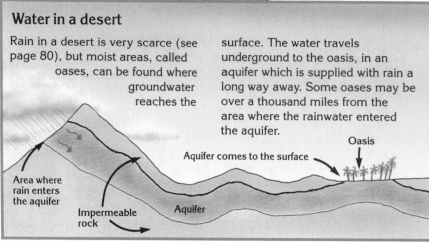

Area where rain enters the aquifer
Impermeable rock
Aquifer
Aquifer comes to the surface
Oasis

Travellers in deserts often make long journeys to an oasis to collect food and water.

Limestone caves

Ground water, like surface water, can weather and erode rock. It is slightly acidic, having absorbed carbon dioxide both from the air and from the soil it has passed through. Limestone is particularly affected by ground water. As it passes along cracks and joints, the water dissolves the limestone, eating away at it and enlarging the cracks.

The cracks gradually widen, allowing water to flow as underground streams. The streams erode the limestone further by processes of river erosion (see pages 74–75).

The process causes areas of rock to collapse, leaving interconnected tunnels and caves within the limestone. Some water evaporates, leaving the minerals which were dissolved in it. These form features such as stalactites and stalagmites (see below).

Testing for carbonates

Any substance containing a carbonate (a chemical substance containing carbon and oxygen) will be dissolved by an acid. Limestone contains calcium carbonate, so it is eaten away by ground water.

To test for carbonates, you will need an old eyedrop dropper or an empty ball point pen tube (stick some tape over the tiny hole in the side), some vinegar (which contains acetic acid), a dish and some substances to test, such as rocks, chalk, sea shells or old snail shells.

Shell

Pen tube

Vinegar

Dish

What to do

1. Put a test ▶ sample in the dish. Dip the dropper or empty pen tube into the vinegar (put your thumb over the top end of the tube – this will hold the vinegar in).

Drop of vinegar

◀ 2. Move the dropper or tube over your sample. If you are using a tube, lightly release your thumb, so the tube acts like a dropper. Let small drops of vinegar drip onto your sample.

Be careful not to let too much vinegar drip out at once.

3. Watch your sample carefully. If it contains a carbonate, it will give off fizzy bubbles of carbon dioxide.

Carbon dioxide bubbles

Fizzing shows the presence of a carbonate.

Stalagmites and stalactites

Water is always dripping down from cracks in the roof of a cave or passage. It contains dissolved minerals, such as calcite. Each drop leaves a tiny ring of calcite on the rock as it falls. The ring grows as more drops fall, and becomes a hollow tube. If it gets blocked, water trickles down the outside of this tube and a stalactite gradually forms as it thickens.

The water which falls to the floor may evaporate, leaving a deposit of calcite which slowly grows up to form a stalagmite. Eventually a stalactite and stalagmite may meet, forming a pillar.

Chimney

Formation of a stalactite

Crack

Drop containing dissolved minerals

The drop deposits a ring of calcite.

The tube grows as more calcite is deposited.

Passage

The tube becomes blocked and calcite is deposited on the outside, forming a stalactite.

If the tube does not become blocked, fine straw stalactites are formed.

Cave

Stalagmite

Pillar

Blocks of limestone where a roof has collapsed

Stalactite

Underground stream

The work of the sea

The waves of the sea have a powerful erosive effect on shores. Some shores are rocky, with high cliffs, others combine rocks with sand, shingle (small pebbles) or large pebbles. The breaking waves smash debris against the cliffs and also move sand and pebbles along the shore. The area between the high and low tide marks shows the greatest amount of damage.

The tides are caused by the pull of the Moon's force of gravity on the Earth.

There are two low tides every day.

High tides occur between low tides.

Longshore drift

Lines of waves usually approach a beach at an angle. This leads to a process called longshore drift. Sand and shingle are picked up, moved along the beach in a zigzag path and deposited elsewhere.

Lines of waves approach the shore.

Direction of the waves

Movement of the sand and shingle

Waves

Most waves are caused by the wind, as it travels over the surface of the sea. The size of a wave depends on the speed of the wind, the time it has been blowing and the distance of open water it has blown across.

In the open sea, the water travels in a circular pattern, making waves.

Crest

Near the shore, the sea becomes shallow and the waves slow down. Their shape changes to an ellipse.

Direction of movement

Trough

The sea becomes too shallow for the wave to complete its full rotation and the top of the wave breaks.

As the wave slows down, it curves over and crashes onto the shore.

Erosion by waves

Waves are the main force of erosion on shores. As they approach a shore, they pick up debris from the sea floor and hurl it against the shore or cliff face. If the rock of a cliff face contains cracks, air is squeezed, or compressed, into them as the waves break. As the waves retreat, the pressure is released and the air pushes back out, shattering the rock. This is called hydraulic action. Debris is gradually broken down and rounded by the repeated action of the waves.

The continuous blasting action of the waves enlarges cracks and joints in a cliff face. eventually forming caves.

Headlands are formed by areas of resistant rock, which have been eroded more slowly than the surrounding, non-resistant rock.

A stack forms if the top of an arch collapses.

Stack

An arch is formed as waves erode caves on both sides of a headland.

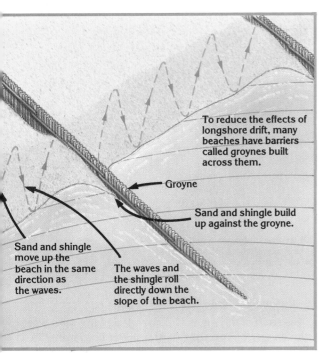

To reduce the effects of longshore drift, many beaches have barriers called groynes built across them.

Groyne

Sand and shingle build up against the groyne.

Sand and shingle move up the beach in the same direction as the waves.

The waves and the shingle roll directly down the slope of the beach.

Spits

Waves also help to build features along the shore. For instance, where the coast changes direction, or at a river mouth, longshore drift carries material straight on, off the edge of the beach. If the material is not carried away by strong currents, a ridge of sand and pebbles, called a spit, is gradually built up.

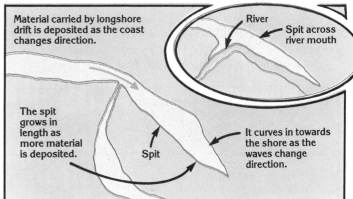

Material carried by longshore drift is deposited as the coast changes direction.

River

Spit across river mouth

The spit grows in length as more material is deposited.

It curves in towards the shore as the waves change direction.

Spit

Estuaries

An estuary is the tidal area where a river reaches the sea. Large areas of mud, deposited by the slow-moving river, are exposed at low tide, but covered at high tide. As the fresh water mixes with salty sea water, the salt makes clay particles in the sediment cling together. They become heavy and are deposited on the mud banks.

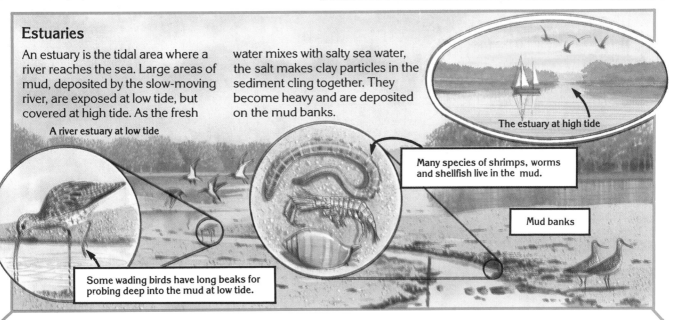

A river estuary at low tide

The estuary at high tide

Many species of shrimps, worms and shellfish live in the mud.

Mud banks

Some wading birds have long beaks for probing deep into the mud at low tide.

Fresh and salt water experiment

As a river reaches the sea, any remaining sediment is deposited due to it slowing down, but also because of the action of the salt in sea water (see above). This experiment shows how salty water speeds up deposition.

1. Put equal amounts of soil into the bottom of two glasses. Fill each glass with water.

Glass   **Water**

Soil

2. Add two teaspoonfuls of salt to one of the glasses.

Stir both mixtures well

Teaspoon

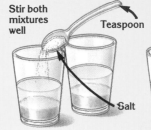

Salt

3. Leave both glasses to stand. The salty water mixture will clear in a few minutes, leaving a layer of sediment on the bottom.

Particles of soil remain suspended in the fresh water.

Salty water

Sediment

Deserts

Deserts are dry, barren areas where less than 10 in. of rain falls each year and the wind is the main factor in shaping the landscape. Not all deserts are hot — some of the world's coldest places are deserts. Desert plants and animals have special ways of coping with the conditions.

Where deserts are found

There are a number of reasons why some areas of the Earth's surface receive little or no rain.

Some deserts, such as the Atacama desert in Chile, are found on the sheltered side of high mountains, called the rainshadow.

Water vapor condenses

Air forced to rise.

Moist, onshore winds

Rain or snow falls on mountains.

Dry winds

Mountain range

Desert

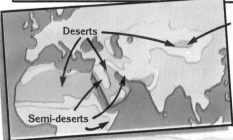

Deserts

Semi-deserts

Other deserts, such as the Gobi desert, are found in the interior of large continents.

Winds lose all their moisture as they travel over land.

Frozen deserts

Most of the snow in Antarctica and the Arctic falls at the coast, whereas areas of the interior receive very little, making them deserts. The snowfall is not very regular and most of the annual amount may fall during one blizzard. The snow has taken thousands of years to build up.

Most polar animals live near the sea, which is their food source.

Thick layers of fat or fur retain their body heat in the extreme cold.

Hot deserts

Hot deserts have a variety of different surfaces. Only some are covered in sand. Others have stones, gravel or bare rock, or a mixture.

Resistant rock

Layers of rock of different resistance

Direction of the prevailing wind

Wind action

There is little to protect a desert from the action of the wind. Strong winds pick up fine surface debris and blast it against exposed rock.

Most erosion takes place just above the surface, where the wind carries most debris.

Mushroom-shaped rock called a zeugen

In sandy deserts, the wind moves sand along the surface and builds ridges called dunes. The shape of a dune depends on the direction of the wind and the size of the sand grains.

The most common dunes are called barchans. They are crescent-shaped.

They are formed in deserts where the wind usually blows in the same direction.

Wind direction

They advance slowly as the sand moves up the gentle slope and is carried over the top of the dune.

They may be up to 100 ft. high.

Seif dunes are long ridges of sand, formed when the wind blows from two directions.

They may be up to 62 mi. long and 328 ft. high.

Wind directions

Temperatures

During the day, surface temperatures in hot deserts may reach 126°F, because there are no clouds to shield the surface from the Sun. It is much cooler underground, so many animals retreat into burrows during the day. At night, temperatures fall very fast, as there are no clouds to trap the heat and prevent it being radiated into space.

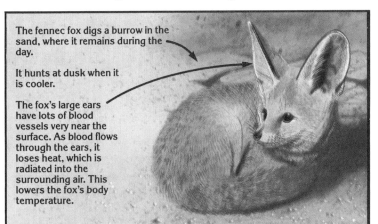

The fennec fox digs a burrow in the sand, where it remains during the day.

It hunts at dusk when it is cooler.

The fox's large ears have lots of blood vessels very near the surface. As blood flows through the ears, it loses heat, which is radiated into the surrounding air. This lowers the fox's body temperature.

Rain in deserts

Although hot deserts receive little rain, there may be occasional short periods of heavy rainfall. The water does not soak in straight away, but runs rapidly across the surface, sweeping up valley debris and carrying it along in channels called wadis.

Some desert plants produce seeds which stay buried for months or even years. After rain has fallen, they grow very quickly into plants. They flower and produce seeds, and then die off as conditions become too dry again.

When it rains, the desert is often scattered with bright flowers.

The seeds survived the dry conditions by lying dormant, or inactive, in the ground.

Many desert plants have a network of shallow roots which spread out over a wide area. The roots absorb any rain which soaks into the ground. The leaves are always very small, to minimise water evaporation from their surfaces.

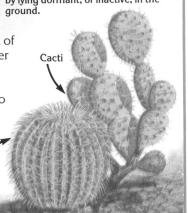

Cacti

Cactus leaves are sharp spines. Their size and shape minimises evaporation and their sharpness prevents them becoming food for desert animals.

When it does rain, cacti can store up the water in their fleshy tissues.

Making a gerbilarium

Gerbils are desert animals which make popular pets. If you or a friend have gerbils, you could build a gerbilarium for them to live in.

Most pet gerbils come from the Mongolian desert, which is hot in summer and cold in winter.

Long legs allow them to cover large areas of land in search of food. They eat mainly seeds, stems and leaves.

Their long tail is used to give them balance when running and jumping.

In the desert, gerbils dig a complex system of burrows, to protect them from the very hot and cold temperatures and from predators.

Fur on the pads of their feet gives protection from the hot surface and also prevents them sinking into the sand.

Feed your gerbils on a diet of mixed seeds and occasionally fresh vegetables.

Keep your gerbils at room temperature, away from drafts and direct sunlight.

Do not disturb the gerbils in their nest.

Use a large aquarium with a tightly-fitting wire-mesh lid for good air circulation.

Put in dry peat moss, mixed with some straw, for the gerbils to burrow in.

Fix a drinking bottle inside the glass and change the water daily.

Sucker

Small leafless branch for climbing and gnawing.

Minimum 8 in.

For bedding, put in clean paper for your gerbils to shred.

The living world

The non-living environment (such things as the atmosphere, water, soil and rock), supports a wealth of living things. Different plants and animals, together with their environment, make up different ecosystems, such as deserts, temperate woodlands or tropical rain forests.

Everything in an ecosystem depends upon everything else for its survival, and each ecosystem depends on all the others. They combine to form the largest ecosystem, the Earth itself.

Food chains

All plants and animals need to break down food inside them, to give them energy for living and growing. Green plants take in the Sun's energy and use it to make their own food in a process called photosynthesis. Animals cannot do this, so instead they have to eat plants or other animals.

In any given ecosystem, the living things are linked by food chains. Plants are the first link in every chain. They are called producers, and are food for plant-eating animals (herbivores), which are called primary consumers.

An animal is called a secondary consumer if it eats herbivores and a tertiary consumer if it eats secondary consumers.

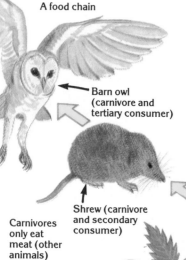

A food chain

Barn owl (carnivore and tertiary consumer)

Shrew (carnivore and secondary consumer)

Carnivores only eat meat (other animals)

Caterpillar (herbivore and primary consumer)

Green plants (producers)

Decomposers

In any food chain there are also decomposers, which feed on dead plant and animal matter. They cause it to break down, or decay (rot), producing various nutrients which enter the soil.

Bacteria, fungi and some insects are decomposers.

Studying decomposers at work

The main decomposers are bacteria and fungi. The air is full of bacteria, and the microscopic seed-like particles of fungi, called spores. You can try an experiment which shows that they are all around you, and in what conditions they will grow.

What to do

1. Put a slice of fresh bread on a table for a few minutes, to collect bacteria and spores. Cut it into four pieces.

2. Place one piece in each of three clear plastic bags (labelled B, C and D) and tightly seal the bags.

Plastic bags

Fresh bread exposed to the air.

3. Dry out the last piece in a hot, sunny place indoors. Place bag B in a warm room, C in a fridge and D in a freezer.

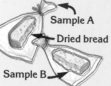

Sample A

Dried bread

Sample B

4. When the sample left out in the sun feels dry and hard, place it in bag A and place it beside sample B.

5. Observe your samples over a period of at least a week. You will find the spores grow best in moist, warm conditions.

Sample A   Sample B   Sample D

Sample C

The very dry and very cold (freezer) bread should show the least growth of bacteria or fungal mold.

Destroying ecosystems

When part of an ecosystem is changed or destroyed, other parts may be affected. If the primary consumer is lost from a food chain, for example, the secondary and tertiary consumers may die out due to lack of food, and the producer (plants) will spread rapidly.

All over the Earth, ecosystems are being destroyed, for example as land is cleared for farming or building. The destruction of ecosystems is causing world-wide concern.

For example, rain forests contain the largest number of insect and plant species in any ecosystem. They are being cut down at an alarming rate and many thousands of species are in danger of extinction.

Food webs

There are many different food chains in every ecosystem. They interlink because each individual species usually eats more than one kind of food. The linking food chains form complex food webs.

A rain forest food web

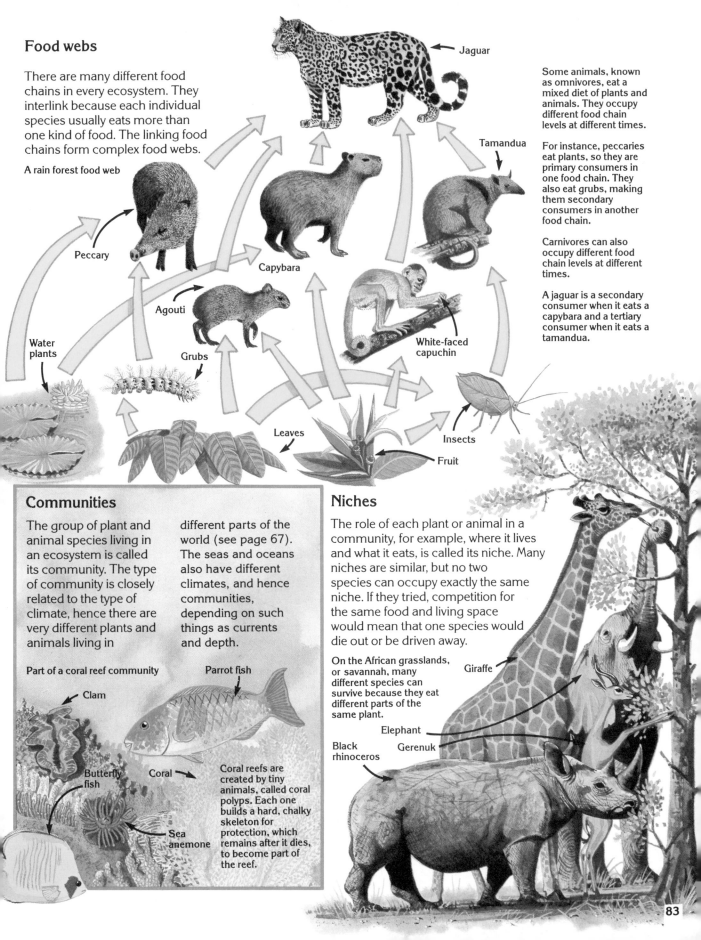

Jaguar

Tamandua

Peccary

Capybara

Agouti

Grubs

White-faced capuchin

Water plants

Leaves

Insects

Fruit

Some animals, known as omnivores, eat a mixed diet of plants and animals. They occupy different food chain levels at different times.

For instance, peccaries eat plants, so they are primary consumers in one food chain. They also eat grubs, making them secondary consumers in another food chain.

Carnivores can also occupy different food chain levels at different times.

A jaguar is a secondary consumer when it eats a capybara and a tertiary consumer when it eats a tamandua.

Communities

The group of plant and animal species living in an ecosystem is called its community. The type of community is closely related to the type of climate, hence there are very different plants and animals living in different parts of the world (see page 67). The seas and oceans also have different climates, and hence communities, depending on such things as currents and depth.

Part of a coral reef community

Parrot fish

Clam

Butterfly fish

Coral

Sea anemone

Coral reefs are created by tiny animals, called coral polyps. Each one builds a hard, chalky skeleton for protection, which remains after it dies, to become part of the reef.

Niches

The role of each plant or animal in a community, for example, where it lives and what it eats, is called its niche. Many niches are similar, but no two species can occupy exactly the same niche. If they tried, competition for the same food and living space would mean that one species would die out or be driven away.

On the African grasslands, or savannah, many different species can survive because they eat different parts of the same plant.

Giraffe

Elephant

Gerenuk

Black rhinoceros

The human population

Nowadays, there are more people living on the Earth than ever before. People create demands on the Earth and its resources, and have altered the natural environment to suit their needs.

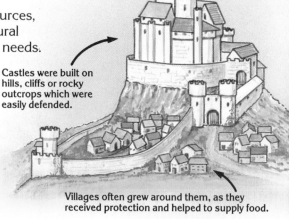

Castles were built on hills, cliffs or rocky outcrops which were easily defended.

Villages often grew around them, as they received protection and helped to supply food.

The effect of the landscape

Since early times, people's lives have been influenced by the landforms and natural environment of an area. People settled in permanent communities in places where they could find water, food and a safe place to live. Many communities began near rivers, springs, wells or oases, or in areas which would not flood. Fertile soils and natural resources, such as coal, also encouraged people to settle.

Population distribution

If all the Earth's surface was suitable to live on, there would be plenty of room for everyone. Large areas are unsuitable, however, so the world's population is unevenly distributed over the land of each continent. Few people live where the climate is too hot or too cold, the area is too mountainous or the soil is unsuitable for farming. Nowadays, most of the world's population lives in cities, towns or villages.

Houses in Indonesia are built on stilts to protect them from flooding during the rainy season.

Some people live in areas where they have had to adapt to unsuitable landscapes or climate.

Despite steep gradients, people in many countries have settled in mountain areas.

They cut terraces in the steep slopes to provide flat areas for planting crops.

A place to live

As the world's population grows, there is more demand for living space. It is estimated that the world's human population will grow to over 6 billion by the year 2000, compared to about 4 billion in 1980. In countries with large fast-growing populations, more people are being forced to live in overcrowded conditions or unsuitable places, such as on the islands in the Ganges delta (see page 75) or on boats in Hong Kong.

Hong Kong is so overcrowded that thousands of people live on boats in the harbor.

City problems

All over the world, people ▶ move from country areas into towns and cities looking for work. This is called urban migration. It causes many problems as the populations of the cities grow rapidly. There may not be enough homes, the streets become too crowded and pollution may increase. Squatter settlements, or shanty towns, may build up on the edges of the cities.

Changing the natural environment

Since early times, people have changed the environment for their own use, for example by clearing land for farming. When the world's population was low, this did not seriously alter ecosystems. But the demands of a growing population have caused great changes.

Natural landscapes and ecosystems have been destroyed to provide land for building cities and transport routes, and to grow more and more crops for food. Huge areas of forest have been destroyed, natural wetlands drained and dry areas watered artificially (irrigated).

Desert area

Irrigation channels

Crops such as dates and figs can be grown in desert areas with the aid of irrigation.

These, and many other actions, have caused great problems. For instance, in many places, cleared land has lost its fertile topsoil through wind or water erosion. This is called soil erosion (see page 71). It leaves unfertile soil, on which less food can be grown. In some areas, soil erosion, combined with drought, has led to famines.

In 1985, 30 million people in Africa were threatened with starvation which was the result of a series of droughts and soil erosion.

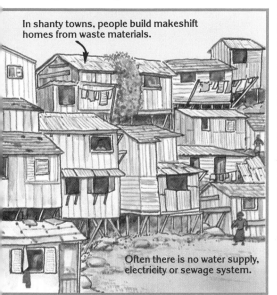

A great deal of their land has been left infertile by over-working and soil erosion.

In shanty towns, people build makeshift homes from waste materials.

Often there is no water supply, electricity or sewage system.

How plants prevent soil erosion

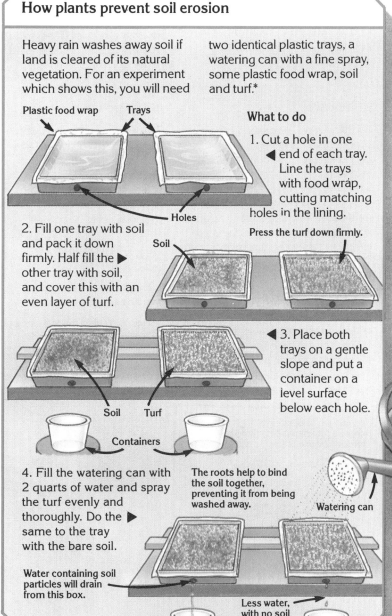

Heavy rain washes away soil if land is cleared of its natural vegetation. For an experiment which shows this, you will need two identical plastic trays, a watering can with a fine spray, some plastic food wrap, soil and turf.*

Plastic food wrap   Trays

Holes

What to do

1. Cut a hole in one end of each tray. Line the trays with food wrap, cutting matching holes in the lining.

Press the turf down firmly.

2. Fill one tray with soil and pack it down firmly. Half fill the other tray with soil, and cover this with an even layer of turf.

Soil

3. Place both trays on a gentle slope and put a container on a level surface below each hole.

Soil   Turf

Containers

4. Fill the watering can with 2 quarts of water and spray the turf evenly and thoroughly. Do the same to the tray with the bare soil.

The roots help to bind the soil together, preventing it from being washed away.

Watering can

Water containing soil particles will drain from this box.

Less water, with no soil

*If you are unable to find some turf, you could grow a tray of cress, but leave it for 12 to 14 days, to allow the roots to bind the soil together.

The Earth's energy resources

Most of the energy we use, for example in homes and industry, is taken from the Earth. For instance, wood is burnt to provide heat and light in many less-developed countries, and fossil fuels, such as coal, oil and gas, are burnt to produce electricity for use in the developed world.

When fossil fuels are used up, they cannot be renewed, or made again, in our lifetime. People are now beginning to investigate energy sources which will not run out.

Fossil fuels

Coal, oil and natural gas are non-renewable energy resources. They were formed from the remains of plants and animals that died millions of years ago. They are taken from the Earth and used in power stations to generate electricity.

The use of fossil fuels as a major source of energy has problems. At the present rate of consumption, known oil and gas reserves could run out within the next fifty years, with coal reserves lasting for about 250 years. Also, burning fossil fuels releases gases which contribute to acid rain and the greenhouse effect.

How fossil fuels were formed

Oil and gas were formed from the remains of microscopic marine plants and animals.

Coal comes from the remains of plants which lived in swamps.

Renewable sources

As the world's population grows and more energy is needed, many countries are developing the use of renewable energy sources – sources which will not run out, such as the Sun, wind and water. The idea is particularly popular because these are "clean" sources, and their use would not damage the environment.

Water power

The force of moving water has been used for centuries to turn water wheels to provide power for various tasks. Nowadays, huge dams and reservoirs are built so that it can be used to generate electricity, called hydro-electricity.

Solar power

The amount of energy which the Earth receives from the Sun is enormous. Modern technology has enabled scientists to develop ways of using this energy to produce solar power.

The world's largest solar power plant is in the Mojave desert in California.

It provides about 2,000 homes with all their energy needs.

The mirrors reflect the Sun's heat to a central boiler, containing water.

The water boils and gives off steam. This drives a turbine, linked to an electricity generator.

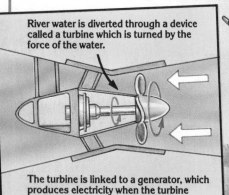

River water is diverted through a device called a turbine which is turned by the force of the water.

The turbine is linked to a generator, which produces electricity when the turbine turns.

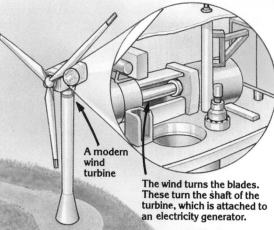

A modern wind turbine

The wind turns the blades. These turn the shaft of the turbine, which is attached to an electricity generator.

Wind energy

The wind has been used as a source of energy for many centuries to power sailing ships and drive machinery. Many different devices have been developed to produce electricity from the wind, or to use the wind's energy in other ways.

Nuclear energy

Nuclear energy is the heat energy released when tiny particles, or atoms, are broken apart. It is used to produce electricity. Uranium, a mineral found in the Earth's crust, is the main fuel used to produce nuclear energy. Many people think nuclear energy could be the main source of power in the future, but there are many problems attached to its use.

Nuclear power stations do not produce polluting gases. But nuclear power can cause several other major environmental problems, as nuclear fuels are radioactive. This means that they give off radiation which kills living things if they are exposed to it. Its effects may be disastrous if it is released into the atmosphere or into the ground.

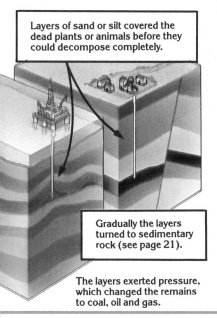

Layers of sand or silt covered the dead plants or animals before they could decompose completely.

Gradually the layers turned to sedimentary rock (see page 21).

The layers exerted pressure, which changed the remains to coal, oil and gas.

There is great concern about nuclear accidents and the disposal of radioactive waste from nuclear power plants.

The nuclear accident in 1986 at Chernobyl, in the USSR, exposed many people and thousands of miles of land to harmful radiation.

Radioactive waste may remain dangerous for thousands of years.

It used to be dumped at sea, but most is now buried underground.

Strong underground vaults

Making a Savonius rotor

The Savonius rotor is a wind machine which is used by farmers in Africa and Asia to pump water for irrigation. To make your own rotor, you will need some thumbtacks, a large plastic bottle, a plastic jar lid, two thread spools, 40 in. length of 5mm dowel and two eyehooks.

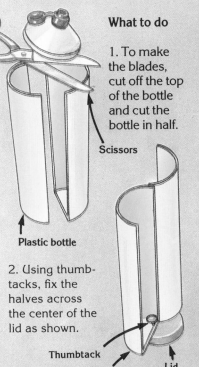

What to do

1. To make the blades, cut off the top of the bottle and cut the bottle in half.

Scissors

Plastic bottle

2. Using thumbtacks, fix the halves across the center of the lid as shown.

Thumbtack

Bottle

Lid

Take care when pushing the thumbtacks into the lid.

3. Stick the thread spools to the base of the lid and push the dowel into them.

Lid

Dowel

Thread spools

4. Screw the eyehooks into a wooden support post where your rotor will catch the wind. Put the dowel through the hooks and test your rotor. Move the position of the bottle halves if necessary.

Support post

Once you have found the best position for the bottle halves, stick them to the lid using strong, waterproof glue.

Other renewable energy sources

In the future, many different natural sources of energy may be used to generate power. For instance, technology to make use of geothermal energy (heat energy from rocks within the Earth) is being developed in volcanic areas. Another source is biogas, a gas formed by rotting waste. It can be burnt to heat buildings and water.

Tidal power is already being developed.

Barrages are built across estuaries.

Reversible turbines generate electricity as the tide rises and falls.

Antarctica

Antarctica is a huge, cold continent, almost twice the size of Australia. It is the only place on Earth which remains relatively unspoilt by humans.

Most of the land is covered by thick ice, though coastal areas are exposed in summer and, further inland, a number of high mountain peaks are permanently ice-free. A variety of wildlife has adapted to living in the freezing conditions.

The frozen continent

Antarctica is the coldest and driest continent on Earth. Over 99% of it is covered by thick ice, up to three miles deep. The center of the continent is a frozen desert (see page 80), where the annual snowfall averages between 1 in. and 2¾ in. and temperatures range from –58°F to –76°F. Areas near the coast are warmer, with more snow, strong winds and temperatures between 14°F to –4°F. In summer, the ice around the coast melts, revealing narrow strips of rocky shoreline, as well as the islands around the coast.

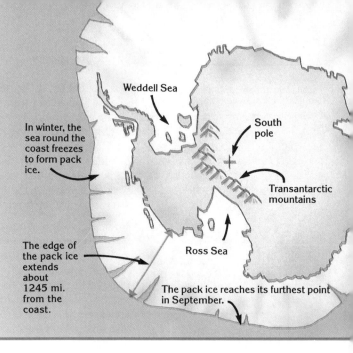

In winter, the sea round the coast freezes to form pack ice.

Weddell Sea

South pole

Transantarctic mountains

Ross Sea

The edge of the pack ice extends about 1245 mi. from the coast.

The pack ice reaches its furthest point in September.

Research in Antarctica

Scientists from many countries work in research stations in Antarctica, and on the islands around its coast. They study many different aspects of the continent, such as its weather, ecosystems, geography and geology.

They also monitor changes in the world's climates, levels of air pollution and the hole in the ozone layer above Antarctica.

Records of weather conditions are made daily by instruments attached to a hydrogen-filled balloon.

They measure temperature, air pressure and humidity over 12½ mi. above Antarctica.

Wildlife

The various birds and other animals which live in Antarctica need to be able to survive the freezing conditions on both the land, where they live and breed, and in the sea, which they depend upon to supply them with their food. They keep in their body heat with either a dense layer of fat, called blubber, found beneath their skin, or with very thick fur.

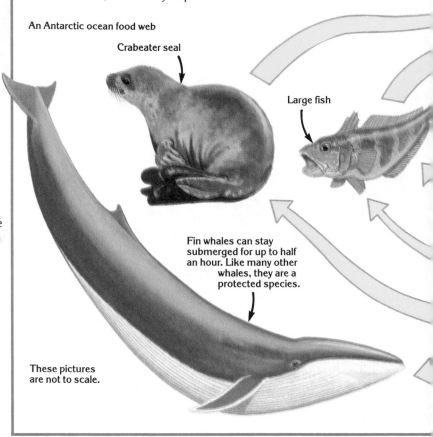

An Antarctic ocean food web

Crabeater seal

Large fish

Fin whales can stay submerged for up to half an hour. Like many other whales, they are a protected species.

These pictures are not to scale.

The Antarctic treaty

In the past, explorers landed in Antarctica and claimed parts of it for their own country. This led to disputes about which country owned which part. In 1959, a treaty was signed by twelve nations who had decided to work together to keep Antarctica free from exploitation. They have now been joined by many other countries.

Antarctica is the only part of the world ruled by an international agreement.

The treaty has helped to protect Antarctica's wildlife.

The scientists from one country must share their discoveries with all the other countries in the treaty.

The only military personnel allowed are those helping at scientific research stations.

Scientists use snowmobiles to travel across the ice.

Mineral exploitation

Geologists think there may be large reserves of minerals, such as coal, iron and copper, in and around Antarctica. Some countries wanted to be given permission to dig there for minerals, but the Antarctic treaty was reviewed in 1991, and any mineral exploration was prevented for fifty years.

Conservationists think that mining for minerals would endanger the animals and plants.

Airstrips and quays would be built in areas which are ice-free in summer.

These are the places where most seal, penguin and seabird colonies are found.

Greenpeace in Antarctica

Greenpeace, the environmental group, has its own research base in Antarctica. Along with many other groups, it is concerned about the future of the continent.

Greenpeace's aim is to make Antarctica a world park, with the plants and animals protected and human activities limited and controlled. They think scientific research should continue, but they are campaigning against mineral exploration and the use of Antarctica for military purposes.

Greenpeace workers in Antarctica are constantly fighting to protect its natural ecosystems.

For instance, they have protested against the construction of an airstrip and collected trash left lying around a research base, which they delivered to the base commander. They are also continuing their fight against whaling.

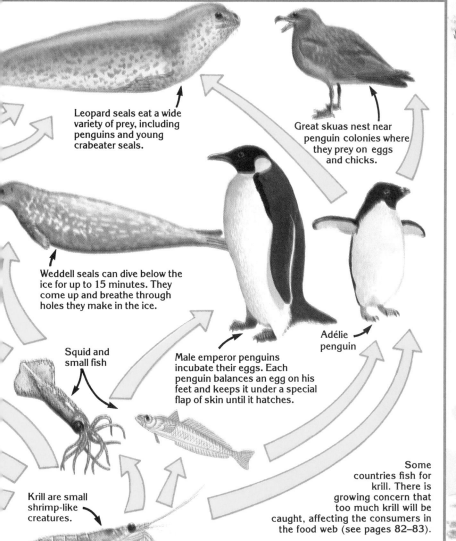

Leopard seals eat a wide variety of prey, including penguins and young crabeater seals.

Great skuas nest near penguin colonies where they prey on eggs and chicks.

Weddell seals can dive below the ice for up to 15 minutes. They come up and breathe through holes they make in the ice.

Squid and small fish

Adélie penguin

Male emperor penguins incubate their eggs. Each penguin balances an egg on his feet and keeps it under a special flap of skin until it hatches.

Krill are small shrimp-like creatures.

Some countries fish for krill. There is growing concern that too much krill will be caught, affecting the consumers in the food web (see pages 82–83).

Controlling the future

In some ways, it is difficult to tell what will happen to the Earth in the future. Natural events and disasters, such as earthquakes, floods and hurricanes are hard to predict accurately.

There are, however, many present-day environmental problems, such as global warming, which have been caused directly by man's activities. In these cases, we are able to predict the disastrous effects of allowing these to continue. We must act together to solve them if the planet is going to be a pleasant place in the future.

World problems

When the world's human population was much smaller, the Earth's natural resources could be exploited without affecting the environment. But now the population is growing so quickly that the demand for fuel, food and shelter is causing serious problems.

Acid rain, soil erosion, rain forest destruction and the threat of global warming are only a few of today's environmental problems. Much can be done to reduce or even solve them, but it will need the co-operation of people and governments around the world.

There are many ways in which action on a large-scale will help the environment.

For instance, if the destruction of rain forests, woodlands and marshes is stopped, many wildlife ecosystems will be preserved.

If there is a decrease in the number of motor vehicles on the roads, there will be less air pollution.

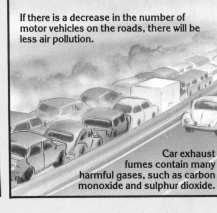

Car exhaust fumes contain many harmful gases, such as carbon monoxide and sulphur dioxide.

You can play your part in improving your environment. For instance, you could put your glass and paper waste into bottle and paper banks for recycling.

Recycling waste reduces the amount of resources taken from the Earth.

The oceans

In the future, the oceans are likely to become a major source of food and energy, so we need to preserve ocean ecosystems and halt the damage that is being done. At the moment, enormous amounts of household and industrial waste are being dumped directly into the water. Spillages from oil tankers are also adding to the pollution.

Cleaning up the pollution is vital if the fish and other sea creatures are to survive. Without them, there will be no food from the sea in the future.

At the same time, the quantities of fish which are caught will need to be carefully controlled to protect natural ecosystems.

Farming

As the world's population grows, so does the demand for food. Many international charities are helping to improve farming techniques in developing countries, which are often those with the fastest-growing populations. They have set up programs to help farmers produce more food from the same area of land, which helps avoid destroying natural ecosystems.

Some new farmland has been created in desert border land. This land once had trees and shrubs, but turned into desert, a process called desertification, because of soil erosion (see page 85) due to overgrazing and the felling of trees, and unfavorable climate conditions, such as droughts and dry winds.

With the aid of irrigation, desert land can be reclaimed to grow crops.

The people grow crops, instead of relying on grazing animals for their food.

Irrigation in the desert has some problems. For instance, the water evaporates quickly in the heat, leaving salt deposits which make the soil too salty for some plants.

Making a model irrigation system

In many irrigation systems, devices called Persian wheels are used to divert water. For a model wheel, you need three plastic lids, 15 Popsicle sticks, a plastic egg box, strong waterproof glue, a cardboard tube from a paper towel roll, three pieces of wood (8 in. x 2 in. x 1 in., 8 in. x 6 in. x ⅜ in. and 4 in. x 1½ in. x 1½ in.), putty, two pieces of 3mm wooden dowel (8 in. and 9 in.), four ⅛ in. cable clips and some foil.

Ask an adult to help you make holes in the lids and hammer in the clips.

What to do

1. Make a hole in the center of one of the lids, so the dowel will fit tightly. Glue 6 Popsicle sticks to the lid, evenly spaced, and push the 8 in. dowel into the hole.

2. To make the wheel, cut up the egg box so you have six cups. Glue one cup to each stick as shown.

3. Cut the cardboard tube in half to make a gutter. Cover it with foil to make it waterproof.

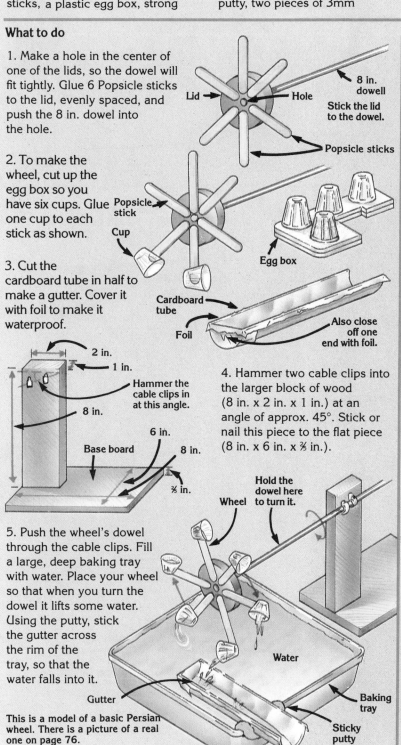

Lid → Hole

8 in. dowell
Stick the lid to the dowel.

Popsicle sticks

Popsicle stick

Cup

Egg box

Cardboard tube

Foil

Also close off one end with foil.

4. Hammer two cable clips into the larger block of wood (8 in. x 2 in. x 1 in.) at an angle of approx. 45°. Stick or nail this piece to the flat piece (8 in. x 6 in. x ⅜ in.).

2 in.
1 in.
Hammer the cable clips in at this angle.
8 in.
6 in.
Base board
8 in.
⅜ in.

5. Push the wheel's dowel through the cable clips. Fill a large, deep baking tray with water. Place your wheel so that when you turn the dowel it lifts some water. Using the putty, stick the gutter across the rim of the tray, so that the water falls into it.

Hold the dowel here to turn it.
Wheel
Water
Gutter
Baking tray
Sticky putty

This is a model of a basic Persian wheel. There is a picture of a real one on page 76.

6. In an irrigation system, a Persian wheel is usually driven by an animal. It turns a drive wheel, linked to the Persian wheel by a gearing system (gear wheel). To make such a gearing system, make two more 6-spoked wheels.

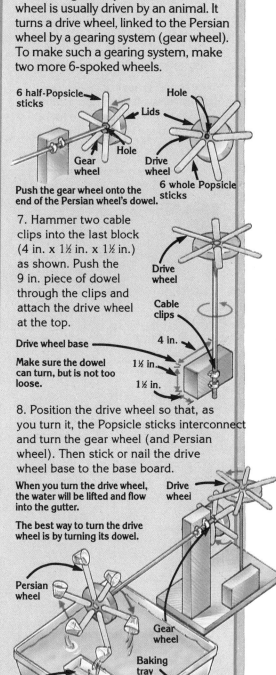

6 half-Popsicle sticks
Hole
Lids
Hole
Gear wheel
Drive wheel
6 whole Popsicle sticks

Push the gear wheel onto the end of the Persian wheel's dowel.

7. Hammer two cable clips into the last block (4 in. x 1½ in. x 1½ in.) as shown. Push the 9 in. piece of dowel through the clips and attach the drive wheel at the top.

Drive wheel

Cable clips

4 in.

Drive wheel base

Make sure the dowel can turn, but is not too loose.

1½ in.
1½ in.

8. Position the drive wheel so that, as you turn it, the Popsicle sticks interconnect and turn the gear wheel (and Persian wheel). Then stick or nail the drive wheel base to the base board.

When you turn the drive wheel, the water will be lifted and flow into the gutter.

Drive wheel

The best way to turn the drive wheel is by turning its dowel.

Persian wheel

Gear wheel

Baking tray

Gutter

Earth facts

The Earth is not a true sphere. It is slightly flattened at the poles. The distance around the Greenwich meridian (see below) is estimated to be 24,861 mi., whereas around the equator it is 24,903 mi.

The total area of the Earth's surface is estimated to be 197 million square miles. The area covered by water is approximately 140 million square miles.

Lines of longitude are imaginary lines which run through the north and south poles. They are used on maps and charts to measure distance in degrees east or west of the Greenwich meridian.

Lines of latitude are imaginary lines which run around the Earth, parallel to the equator. They are used on maps and charts to measure distance in degrees north or south of the equator.

North pole

Lines of longitude

Equator
(latitude 0°)

Lines of latitude

South pole

Greenwich meridian
(longitude 0°)

The highest temperature was recorded in Libya in 1922 (136.4°F).

The highest point on the Earth's surface is Mount Everest (29,021½ ft.).

Asia

Europe

North America

Atlantic Ocean

Pacific Ocean

Pacific Ocean

Africa

Equator

Indian Ocean

The Pacific Ocean covers more area than all the land surface put together.

South America

Australia

Atlantic Ocean

Key

Mountains

Deserts

Tropical rain forests

Antarctica

The longest river is the Nile in Africa (4,144¾ mi. in length).

The place with the greatest recorded rainfall in twenty-four hours is the Island of Réunion (73.62 in.).

The longest glacier is the Lambert glacier in Antarctica (approximately 248.56 mi. in length).

Useful addresses

Below are some addresses of museums which have departments with permanent displays of rocks, fossils, wildlife etc. Your local library may be able to help you find addresses of smaller, local museums or suggest geological features in your area which you can visit. Also included are the main international addresses of some organizations concerned with the Earth and its natural environments. They may be able to provide you with further information.

International organizations

World-Wide Fund for Nature International,
Information Division,
Avenue Mont-Blanc,
CH-1196 Gland,
Switzerland

Friends of the Earth International,
26-28 Underwood Street,
London N1 7JQ

Greenpeace International,
Keizersgracht 176,
1016 DW Amsterdam,
The Netherlands

United Kingdom

The Natural History Museum,
(including The Geological Museum),
Cromwell Road,
London SW7 5BD

The Royal Scottish Museum,
Chambers Street,
Edinburgh EH1 1JF

National Museum of Wales,
Cathays Park,
Cardiff CF1 3NP

Leeds City Museum,
Municipal Buildings,
Leeds,
Yorks LS1 3AA

Manchester Museum,
The University,
Oxford Road,
Manchester MI3 9PL

City Museum and Art Gallery,
Department of Natural History,
Chamberlain Square,
Birmingham B3 3DH

United States of America

American Museum of Natural History,
Central Park West and 79th Street,
New York,
NY 10024

Denver Museum of Natural History,
City Park,
Denver,
Colorado 80205

National Museum of Natural History,
Wade Oval,
University Circle,
Cleveland,
Ohio 44106

California Academy of Sciences,
Golden Gate Park,
San Francisco,
CA 9418

Los Angeles Museum of Natural History,
900 Exposition Blvd.,
Exposition Park,
Los Angeles,
CA 90007

National Museum of Natural History,
10th Street and Constitution Ave. NW,
Washington DC 20560

Canada

National Museum of Natural Sciences,
Victoria Memorial Museum Building,
Metcalfe and Mcleod Streets,
Ottawa,
Ontario K1A 0M8

Saskatchewan Museum of Natural History,
Wascana Park,
College Street and Albert Street,
Regina,
Saskatchewan SP4 3V7

Australia and New Zealand

Australian Museum,
6-8 College Street,
Sydney,
New South Wales 2000

S. Australian Museum,
North Terrace,
Adelaide,
South Australia 5000

Queensland Museum,
Cultural Centre,
South Bank,
South Brisbane,
Queensland 4101

Museum of Victoria,
328 Swanston Street,
Melbourne,
Victoria 3000

The Western Australian Museum,
Francis Street,
Perth,
Western Australia 6000

National Museum,
Buckle Street,
Wellington,
New Zealand

Redpath Museum,
856 Sherbrooke Street West,
Montreal,
Quebec H3A 2K6

Royal Ontario Museum,
100 Queen's Park,
Toronto,
Ontario M5S 2C6

Provincial Museum of Alberta,
102nd Avenue,
Edmonton,
Alberta T5N 0M8

Glossary

Aquifer. An area of permeable rock which is capable of holding water and allows water to travel through it.

Astronomer. A scientist who studies the stars, planets and other bodies which make up the Universe.

Atmosphere. The mixture of gases which surrounds the Earth. It has a number of layers.

Backwash. The movement of a wave back down a beach after it has broken (see **Swash**).

Billion. One USA billion = one thousand million (1,000,000,000). This is the value used throughout this book. In some other countries, e.g. the UK, one billion = one million million (1,000,000,000,000).

Climate. The average weather conditions experienced in an area. Climates vary greatly around the world.

Continent. One of the large masses of land into which the Earth's surface is divided. The world's continents are Europe, Asia, Africa, North and South America, Australia and Antarctica.

Continental plates. The massive interlinking pieces which form the surface layer, or crust, of the Earth. They move around in relation to each other.

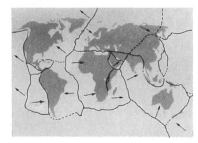

Debris. Fragments formed when weathering and erosion break down the surface of rocks.

Delta. A build-up of sand or silt, which splits up the mouth of a river into a number of channels.

Desert. Any area of the Earth's surface which receives less than 10 in. of rain in a year.

Desertification. The process by which dry areas become deserts. It is a great problem at the edges of deserts where droughts have accelerated the process.

Drought. A long period of time with little or no rain.

Ecosystem. A self-contained system of living and non-living parts, consisting of plants, animals and the environment they live in.

Environment. Everything which surrounds a plant or animal, including the land, the atmosphere and other plants and animals.

Erosion. The wearing away and movement of material on the Earth's surface. The main agents of erosion are the wind, water and ice.

Faults. Cracks (**fractures**) which are lines of weakness in the Earth's crust and along which movement occurs.

Fetch. The stretch of open sea which any particular wind blows across.

Flood plain. A flat area which extends out on both sides of a river channel. It is formed from layers of sediment, deposited when the river overflows its banks.

Folds. Bends in rocks, caused by movements of the Earth's crust.

Food chain. A chain of living organisms which are linked together by their feeding relationships. Energy is passed on through each organism in the chain.

Fossil fuels. Fuels such as coal, oil and natural gas, which are the remains of living matter that died millions of years ago.

Glacier. A mass of moving ice which travels slowly due to the force of gravity.

Global warming. An overall increase in world temperatures, thought to be caused by pollution in the atmosphere effectively increasing the greenhouse effect.

Greenhouse effect. The warming effect caused by gases in the atmosphere trapping the Sun's heat.

Ground water. Water which has seeped into the soil and rock below the surface of the ground.

Humidity. The amount of water vapor in the atmosphere.

Hydro-electric power. Electricity generated by using the force of moving water. Hydro-electric power is one of the most widely used forms of renewable energy.

Ice sheet. A vast mass of ice and snow, sometimes called an ice-cap, which covers a massive area. Ice sheets are found in the Arctic and Antarctica.

Igneous rock. Rock which is formed when molten rock from beneath the Earth's crust cools and hardens.

Impermeable rock. Rock which does not allow water to pass through it easily.

Irrigation. The artificial watering of an area of land in order to create fertile land on which to grow crops.

Lava. Magma which has flowed out onto the Earth's surface.

Magma. Molten (liquid) rock found beneath the Earth's surface.

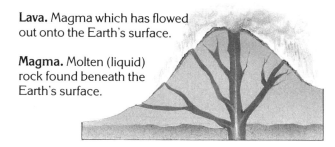

Metamorphic rock. Rock which has been changed from one type of rock into another by great heat or pressure.

Minerals. Naturally-made, non-living substances with a particular chemical make-up. Rocks are composed of one or more different minerals.

Ozone layer. A layer of ozone gas found in the Earth's atmosphere. It absorbs some of the Sun's harmful ultra-violet rays.

Permeable rock. Rock which allows water to pass through it easily. The water travels through spaces between individual rock particles or cracks in the rock.

Precipitation. Any moisture which reaches the Earth from the atmosphere, or forms on the Earth's surface. It includes rain, snow, sleet, hail, dew and frost.

Prey. An animal which is killed and eaten by another animal (the **predator**).

Renewable energy. Energy from sources which are constantly available in the natural world, such as wind, water or the Sun.

Sediment. Rock debris, such as sand, mud or gravel, deposited by the wind, water or ice.

Sedimentary rock. Rock formed from layers of sediment which were deposited and squeezed together.

Solar energy. The energy contained in the Sun's rays which can be converted into electricity using a solar, or photovoltaic, cell.

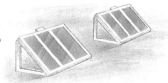

Swash. The movement of a wave as it breaks and advances up a beach (see **Backwash**).

Tornado. A twisting, funnel-shaped cloud, reaching down to the ground. Tornadoes create strong, spiralling winds which may cause severe damage, e.g. to buildings and trees.

Tropical cyclone. A violent tropical storm in which the winds circulate around a central point, or "eye". Tropical cyclones are also known as hurricanes, typhoons or, in Australia, willy-willies.

Tropical grasslands. Vast open areas of grass with a few scattered trees, found in tropical regions. Grasslands are given different names in different locations. For instance, they are called savannahs in East Africa and campos or llanos in South America.

Tsunami. A giant wave caused by an earthquake taking place beneath the ocean. It is sometimes misleadingly called a tidal wave.

Weathering. The disintegration of rocks by various processes due to exposure to the weather.

Index